Power in modern Russia

Manchester University Press

POCKET POLITICS
SERIES EDITOR: BILL JONES

Pocket politics presents short, pithy summaries of complex topics on socio-political issues both in Britain and overseas. Academically sound, accessible and aimed at the interested general reader, the series will address a subject range including political ideas, economics, society, the machinery of government and international issues. Unusually, perhaps, authors are encouraged, should they choose, to offer their own conclusions rather than strive for mere academic objectivity. The series will provide stimulating intellectual access to the problems of the modern world in a user-friendly format.

Previously published
The Trump revolt   Edward Ashbee
Reform of the House of Lords   Philip Norton

Power in modern Russia

Strategy and mobilisation

Andrew Monaghan

Moyre

with best wishes

Andrew

25 Nov 2017

Lewes.

Manchester University Press

The right of Andrew Monaghan to be identified as the author of this work has been asserted by him in accordance with the Copyright, Designs and Patents Act 1988.

Published by Manchester University Press
Altrincham Street, Manchester M1 7JA
www.manchesteruniversitypress.co.uk

British Library Cataloguing-in-Publication Data
A catalogue record for this book is available from the British Library

ISBN   978 1 5261 2641 2 paperback

First published 2017

The publisher has no responsibility for the persistence or accuracy of URLs for any external or third-party internet websites referred to in this book, and does not guarantee that any content on such websites is, or will remain, accurate or appropriate.

Typeset by Out of House Publishing
Printed in Great Britain
by CPI Group (UK) Ltd, Croydon, CR0 4YY

Contents

Acknowledgements

Many debts of thanks have accrued during the preparation and writing of this book. The origins of the idea took shape while I was at the NATO Defence College in Rome, and I would like to thank Dieter Löser, Grant Hammond, Rich Hooker and participants in the Roman Baths Advisory Group for their friendship and support. I also had the pleasure of developing the ideas as an Academic Visitor at St Antony's College, Oxford, and particular thanks go to Alex Pravda and Roy Allison for their support.

Much of the research work was carried out while I was Senior Research Fellow in the Russia and Eurasia Programme at Chatham House, the Royal Institute of International Affairs. I greatly appreciate the generosity of the Gerda Henkel Foundation's Special Programme for Security, Society and the State for the financial support for the project 'Towards Mobilisation: From a Nation in Arms to a Nation Armed' (2015–17). This support facilitated my own research, travel, and a number of workshops and seminars, and I am grateful both to the participants of these sessions for their active contributions and to Lubica Pollakova and Anna Morgan for all their help and support organising the events.

The book itself was written during my time as a Visiting Fellow at the Oxford Programme on the Changing Character of War at Pembroke College, and I very much appreciate the support and encouragement of Rob Johnson, Ruth Murray and the many others I have met through the programme.

Many thanks are due to Amanda Moss at Chatham House, and the editors of the journal *International Affairs* for kind permission to revisit, sew together and develop material already published, including the articles 'The Russian *Vertikal*: The Tandem, Power and the Elections' (2011), 'Defibrillating the Vertical: Putin and Russian Grand Strategy' (2014), and 'Russian State Mobilisation: Moving the Country onto a War Footing' (2016).

I have also been lucky to enjoy the support of numerous librarians. Thanks to Simon Blundell, Richard Ramage at St Antony's, David Bates and his team at Chatham House and the library team in the NATO Defence College for all their courteous help. I am also grateful to my publishers at Manchester University Press, and particularly the series editor, Bill Jones, for their support for the idea of the book and seeing it through to publication.

Many other individuals have influenced the thinking that underpins the book, including discussions with numerous officials in the UK, USA, NATO and in Russia. Others, including David Glantz, Dov Lynch, Nazrin Mehdiyeva, Julian Cooper, Silvana Malle and Henry Plater-Zyberk, have been kind enough to read parts or all of the draft. I am grateful to all for taking the time to discuss these themes with me, and their firm but always gentle corrections. The book is much the better for their advice and wisdom, but where I have failed satisfactorily to incorporate it, and for any remaining errors, I alone am to blame.

In Russia, I have enjoyed many discussions – and much kindness and patience in instructing me – about how to attempt to understand Russia's complexities and nuances. I'm grateful to all those who have taken the time to talk to me. In particular, Ekaterina Vladimirovna's ability to cross cultural divides is exemplary, and Boris Mikhailovich and Mikhail Borisovich have always shown me a warmth and generosity that mentioning here barely acknowledges. They realise, I hope, the extent of my appreciation, and their influence can also be felt throughout this book.

Finally, and as always, my thanks and love go to my family, Charles and Dorothy Monaghan, and to Yulia. Their patience, love and support mean the world to me. I could not have written the book without it. Lara Andreevna's happy presence remains, as always, a bright light in life.

Abbreviations

GUSP	Main Directorate for Special Projects
KGB	Committee of State Security
MChS	Emergencies Ministry
MVD	Ministry of the Interior
NATO	North Atlantic Treaty Organization
NDMC	National Defence Management Centre
NG	National Guard
ONF	All-Russian Popular Front
SC	Security Council
UR	United Russia
VEB	Vneshekonombank

Introduction: strategy in a time of crisis

DOES the Russian leadership have a grand strategy? Is there a coherent and consistent strategic agenda? If so, what is it? What does President Putin have in mind? Is he, indeed, a strategic genius – or is he making it up day-to-day? What will Russia do next? And what are Putin's intentions regarding the West? As French journalists inquired of Putin himself, is Russian strategy 'on a path of dialogue, or expansion and conquest?'[1] Since the sharp deterioration in relations between the Euro-Atlantic community and Russia following the eruption of war in Ukraine in 2014 and Russia's intervention in Syria in 2015, these questions have troubled senior politicians and officials in Western capitals.

Some doubt the idea of a Russian grand strategy. Michael McFaul, a former US ambassador to Russia, is among those who argue that Putin does not know what he wants from the Ukraine crisis, has no grand plan and makes policy up as he goes. Others see him as a tactician, but no strategist. The prominent strategic thinker Lawrence Freedman has argued that although Putin is good at making early moves he has not thought through subsequent developments, and that it is difficult to evaluate what Russian strategy is beyond the most general lines. Indeed, Putin is already failing, according to Freedman, since he is caught in a web in Syria.

Still others have suggested that Putin is a *bad* strategist, since he does not understand the relationship between military violence and political objectives, and is pursuing a self-defeating strategy that is reducing Russian power and leaving it isolated, all but ruining his ambition to return Russia to the ranks of great powers. The UK's House of Foreign Affairs Committee concluded, for instance, that Moscow's approach to foreign policy is opportunistic and tactical, meaning that Russia has been making strategic mistakes and pursuing short-term advantages rather than advancing a long-term, coherent, sustainable vision for its role in the world.[2]

Such sceptics draw on a tradition that doubts Moscow's ability to create strategy, and emphasises the role of contingency, even a tradition of anti-strategy: a Tolstoyan rejection of strategy in which strategic planning is futile because luck plays too great a role and the Russian leadership has too little control over events. Other problems include decision-making processes beset by informality, dysfunction and political infighting. These flaws lead to inconsistent and uncoordinated policies which undermine or even prevent the ability of the Russian leadership to shape a coherent strategy. Celeste Wallander, a prominent US observer who has held senior policy and academic positions, memorably suggested in 2007 that Russian grand strategy is 'neither grand, nor strategic, nor sustainable'.[3]

Nevertheless, the view that Moscow has a strategy, even of Putin as a strategic genius, has become an orthodoxy across the Euro-Atlantic community, and a broad consensus has taken shape around the notions of Putin's complete authority within Russia, his ability to make rapid decisions because of the centralised nature of authority in Russia, and his creation of a 'vertical of power unlike any we have seen in other great nations'.[4]

General Adrian Bradshaw, then NATO's Deputy Supreme Allied Commander, Europe, illustrated this view in March 2017 when he emphasised that NATO was 'grappling with a spectrum of Russian aggression towards the West, from provocative military measures on Europe's borders to subversion alongside a tide of digital propaganda and efforts to manipulate the US presidential election'.[5] Bradshaw's view that Putin 'has his hands on all the levers of power' is widespread among Euro-Atlantic policy-makers and observers, who emphasise Putin's control of all aspects of national power, military and non-military, in a seamless linking of state power. Many see Moscow to have increasingly displayed a real focus on the whole of government, a 'full spectrum approach' that seeks to integrate fully all activities within a strategic design and drawing on all national means to achieve its ends. This is often known as 'hybrid warfare' or the so-called 'Gerasimov Doctrine', based on a simplistic reading of an article published by the Russian Chief of General Staff, Valeriy Gerasimov, in 2013.[6]

Others go further, believing him to be a 'calculating master of geopolitics with a master plan' to divide Europe, destroy NATO, demonstrate that Russia is a global power, and, most of all, marginalise the United States and the West. Putin's actions show a 'consistent logic and strategic coherence', as he foments 'low-level conflict to undermine stability and ultimately promote expanded Russian influence'. Similarly, some suggest that he has launched a 'chaos strategy' and has seized the momentum of the unravelling of the Western order, and, having transformed great weakness into considerable strength, to have launched a kind of 'global imperialist insurgency' such that he is dictating the 'mood of the unfolding era', stirring and guiding the currents of change.[7] For those who emphasise Putin's KGB background, it is axiomatic that the Kremlin has a strategy: an aggressive, expansive, neo-imperialist central Russian strategy to sustain domestic legitimacy and popularity, and exemplify it by pointing to specific Russian foreign policy moves and matching lists of perceived Russian strengths against known and assumed Western weaknesses and failings.

In Russia, the balance of the debate has been with sceptics who point to bureaucratic problems and incompetence, and the dysfunctionality of the Russian system.[8] Ruslan Pukhov, Director of the Centre for Analysis of Strategies and Technologies in Moscow, has suggested that despite some progress since the 1990s, there is only limited consensus on national goals beyond the desire to be a leading independent, global player. Answers to important questions are 'often being given "on the hoof", knee-jerk reactions to whatever challenges, threats or problems the country happens to be facing at any given moment'.[9] Similarly,

Mikhail Zygar, a prominent journalist, suggests that Putin-era Russia 'lacks logic', and that there is an absence of a plan or clear strategy on the part of Putin himself or his courtiers. Everything that happens is a tactical step, a 'real-time response to external stimuli devoid of an ultimate objective'.[10]

Nevertheless, there are many Russians who advocate the importance of grand strategy. The conservative political Izborsky club, for instance, published a manifesto in 2012 entitled 'Mobilisation project – the founding premises of a "major break-through" strategy'.[11] In 2013, Alexander Prokhanov, one of the club's senior figures, asked Putin directly whether there was a 'synthetic, integrated project, a large project, a "Russia project" underway'. Putin replied that Russia is 'not a project, but a destiny', before outlining Russia's development plans to 2020, focusing on the development of the military and infrastructure.[12]

Indeed, Putin and many other senior Russian officials have often stated that Russia has what amounts to a 'unified action programme', one that reflects a strategic agenda set out in 2011 and 2012, and that 'only by mobilising all the resources at our disposal ... will we get results'.[13] And, in response to the direct question posed about whether Russian strategy is one of dialogue or expansion and conquest, Putin stated that it was one of dialogue.

Given the sharp deterioration in relations between the Euro-Atlantic community and Russia, it is important to understand better the question of Russian grand strategy. What does the Russian leadership mean by a 'unified action programme' – and what is implied by the emphasis on military modernisation? What are the problems that Russian observers emphasise and how do they undermine strategy? What do the hints at 'mobilisation' mean – and how do they relate to Russian grand strategy?

This book explores these questions. It argues that the idea of Russian strategy has been poorly understood, partly because of confusion over what strategy means and partly because of a misdiagnosis of a Russian 'master plan' and the notion of the 'seamless coordination' of activities against the Euro-Atlantic community, even the international order. The labels 'Gerasimov

Doctrine' and 'hybrid warfare' reflect a misunderstanding of Russian thinking and actions, at once a partial and simplistic reading and too narrow a focus on specific aspects of Russian activity; indeed, while the concept of 'hybrid warfare' has become fashionable, it pitches an understanding of Russian strategic thinking and making at the wrong level and misses the bigger picture of Russian grand strategy. At the same time, assertions of a Russian 'master plan' often simply amount to joining up some dots of various externally visible activities and deducing that they are driven by a strategic agenda – regardless of the inherent difficulties of strategy-making and any Russian internal complexities.

Furthermore, beyond simplistic assertions that Putin is try-ing to rebuild the USSR or destroy NATO, Moscow's strategic planning, along with the assumptions on which it is based, is usually ignored or dismissed. And the focus on Putin, which all too easily subsides into ill-informed and clichéd 'Putinology', misses much about how Russia works and instead merely reflects the highly politicised nature of the debate about Russia and Euro-Atlantic security since 2014.[14] It is an easy dysphemism to call Putin 'merely' a tactician, and those who emphasise his strategic prowess usually do so to contrast an abstract version of Putin's decisiveness against the weakness of Western leaders or the lack of Western strategy, rather than illuminate any actual Russian strategy.

Examining Russian strategy sheds light both on how Moscow sees the world and how Russia works, and, importantly, does not. The book argues that Russian strategy is less to be found in Moscow's plans, and more in the so-called vertical of power. In so doing, it reveals important shifts underway in the Russian political and security landscape and shapes an argu-ment about a missed diagnosis of Russian state mobilisation.

The argument is framed in two parts. First, the broader picture of Russian grand strategy is examined, reflecting ini-tially on Russian strategic planning under Vladimir Putin and then on the leadership's ability to implement those plans. Since Putin came to power, Moscow has consistently sought to shape strategic planning, but has often struggled with its implementation. Chapters 3 and 4 then turn to look at the measures that the leadership is enacting to attempt to remedy problems and create strategy. Since the turn of this decade, and particularly since the so-called 'Arab Spring', these have appeared as emergency measures to improve the functioning of the system at a time of looming crisis. The most notable aspect of this has been the effort to prepare Russia to face a range of possible threats – to consolidate the body politic and the economy and prepare and enhance the security and military capabilities. Indeed, security concerns have come to dominate Moscow's agenda, such that it appears that the leadership has prepared to move the country onto a war footing.

Some important points are worth registering at the outset, since Russia and the concepts of strategy and mobilisation are all contentious, especially when examined together at a time of high tension. 'Grand strategy' is a term often used but rarely defined in a clear or meaningful way. In the debate about Russia it is often misused, and is seen as synonymous with Moscow's plans, policies or (often nefarious) goals. Difficult though it is to define in a way that will satisfy all, simply put, grand strategy refers to the art of bringing together and using all of the nation's resources to promote the interests of the state, including securing it against enemies perceived and real. It is the relationship between military, economic, political and cultural means and political ends – the art, as Lawrence Freedman has suggested, of creating power.

But this requires some further explanation. Importantly for the book's argument, one point that is universally accepted by strategic thinkers is that strategy is *not* a plan, nor is it a set of goals or objectives. Instead, strategy is the combination of the formulation of plans in theory *and their implementation in practice*: it is an executive function and, without it, even good plans come to nothing or fall apart.

If strategy is a 'bridge' between plans and action, clearly it should be understood with reference to the people and institutions who formulate and implement the plans. Strategy requires the careful coordination and balancing of the various interests of those actors – in effect 'conducting the orchestra', as opposed to playing the individual instruments. In formulating the plans, this requires matching the necessary degree of political flexibility to square and satisfy divergent internal interests and retain adaptability in the face of events with the clarity necessary for those who will implement them. As Freedman has put it, the problem with strategy is other people – both on your own side and adversaries. Successful strategy requires people to follow the script, and as soon as they deviate, then problems emerge.

Similarly, strategy is a process of dialogue with a changing context, of constant adaptation to evolving conditions and circumstances in a world in which chance, uncertainty and ambiguity dominate. This raises two points. First, the assumptions of the leadership play an important role in influencing strategy. Indeed, as Colin Gray has suggested, assumptions underpin the entire strategic architecture of means and ends: how the leadership sees the world drives their attempt to make strategy, their prioritisation and their actions. Assumptions, he says, 'are always likely to be crucially important for action contemplated in the future, since reliable empirical evidence about the consequences of future behaviour is certain to be missing at strategy selection time'.[15]

Second, leaders must balance their resources and attempt to plan for an uncertain future, one that is shrouded in 'fog', while simultaneously dealing with the impact of the 'friction' of events and opposition that warps initial formulations even as they are being implemented. It is, therefore, both an iterative process and an extremely difficult undertaking. Regardless of how well it is done, subsequent events will require the plans to be revised, assumptions to be reconsidered and new routes plotted.

Strategy, then, is summed up by Gray as a concept that 'aspires to provide guidance and control over all the assets of a polity for the purpose of achieving a collective effort to meet the overall challenge of the day'. It is the 'direction and use of any or all of the assets of a security community and, in order to be grand', he continues, 'strategy needs to be capable of mobilising any of a community's assets'.[16] It is about the management and the execution of a 'purposeful set of ideas' about what a nation seeks to accomplish in the world and how it should go about doing so by prioritising finite resources to ensure the security of the state. It requires foresight, despite the fact of uncertainty, and it needs a steadiness of purpose necessary to plan ahead combined with the ability to adapt.[17]

Mobilisation is a similarly difficult term, one that is highly symbolic with many historical and political connotations. It is often seen as reflecting the idea of a 'nation in arms', a Napoleonic *levée en masse*, and the call for mass volunteerism (and conscription) to defend the motherland. It also has connotations of a 'train timetable' type of mobilisation of the kind that took place at the outbreak of the First World War, an administrative process that happens *after* the outbreak of war, in which a country's ability to mobilise is predetermined by logistical structures.

More recently, the term mobilisation has taken on a political flavour, building on traditions with roots in the political left. This understanding has a strong progressive, even revolutionary, feel, related to the emergence of political consciousness and enfranchisement. Indeed, this is how it has usually been applied to Russia (and the other post-Soviet states) in the post-Cold War era, as observers have focused on (democratic) opposition protests mobilising against the (authoritarian) leadership using social media and, to a lesser degree, the attempts of the authorities to counter-mobilise against these protests.

In Russia, although it has some broad historical similarities in terms of volunteerism and conscription in defence of the motherland, and while there is some discussion of contemporary social mobilisation (and counter-mobilisation), *state* mobilisation has a rather different and more specific meaning that is essential to understand for the argument below. It is worth clarifying what is meant here, not least since the argument pursues the line that there is a shift in meaning *away* from traditional forms of mass mobilisation towards a more modern form.

A preliminary point to note is that the term mobilisation is much more prevalent in the public and political debate in Russia than it is in the Euro-Atlantic community. Indeed, in many ways, Western societies are not just demobilised after the end of the Cold War, but increasingly de-*militarised*. In her stimulating book *War Time*, a reflection on the evolving character of war in the twenty-first century, Mary Dudziak has argued that in the United States, a separation has taken place between war-fighting and the wider population. During the lengthy US commitment to fighting in Iraq and Afghanistan, war became 'normal life' for the wider US population – there was no wider call to arms to defend the nation, indeed 'absent was the call to national unity that might be hoped for in wartime'. Rather than sacrificing for the war effort, the population was specifically to continue with daily life. War, she argued, had become the government's task, not something that the population experienced, and war governance has the character of 'bureaucratic management rather than crusade'.[18] In many ways, this reflects the antithesis of traditional mobilisation.

In contrast, in Russia the word 'mobilizatsiya' often features in discussions about contemporary international relations and security, politics and economics, and about whether the international instability and insecurity, with even the looming prospect of war, means that Russians are living in a time of mobilisation. Senior party politicians and prominent officials have spoken publicly of mobilisation as part of Russia's anti-crisis plan, and as the means of consolidating society, improving state administration and responding to a challenging, even threatening, international environment. Mobilisation plans have been prepared by the government. The term featured in Gerasimov's famous 2013 article, and when Turkey shot down a Russian Su-24 bomber in November 2015, the Kremlin announced that, in responding to the challenge, the president was 'fully mobilised'.[19]

The Russian state has a specific definition of mobilisation – 'a complex of state measures for activating the resources, strength and capabilities for the achievement of military-political aims'. It includes practical measures for the transition on to a war footing of the country's military, economic and state institutions at all levels (general mobilisation), or of some part of them (partial mobilisation). Mobilisation can be carried out openly or secretly, and its announcement is the responsibility of the head of state (the president) and the highest organs of state authority. The most important conditions for the successful fulfilment of mobilisation include: having sufficient numbers of trained people to bring units up to strength and create new formations; the provision in peacetime of the necessary arms, equipment, ammunition and fuel; and a clearly structured system for announcing mobilisation and for gathering and distributing the resources associated with it.[20]

Such a definition is very close to that of grand strategy noted above, and provides a clear basis for the discussion below. It is important to note, though, that there are two main pillars of Russian state mobilisation, economic and military. Mobilisation of the economy is the foundation for wider, general mobilisation, and is reflected in the reorganisation and conversion of industry, natural resources, transport and communications to the service of the armed forces, the activities of the state and the needs of the population in times of war. These economic and military aspects of mobilisation have important historical roots which still echo today, but there are fundamental shifts underway in practice.

Mobilisation is based on two stages. The first stage is defined as 'mobilizatsionnaya podgotovka' (mobilisation preparation), which is when an armed conflict could appear and during which state agencies are prepared to deploy forces, mobilise the economy for war and begin negotiating with potential allies and adversaries. If war becomes imminent, the leadership announces the second stage, when it brings all armed forces to full military strength and concentrates and deploys them. This is associated with battle readiness, and today this is known as 'mobilizatsionnaya gotovnost' (mobilisation readiness). These definitions illustrate an important point, one emphasised by Gerasimov in his 2013 article, that mobilisation is understood as a *peacetime activity, in advance of conflict*, a peacetime preparation of the organs of state power, administrative authorities, economy and armed forces to defend the state from armed attack.

A couple of caveats must be made at the outset. First, understanding Russian strategy requires a degree of empathy – in effect, attempting to see the world through Russian eyes. This is not synonymous with 'sympathy', or attempting to argue either for those policies or that disagreements should be overlooked. From the start, therefore, it is important to be clear: the disagreements between the Euro-Atlantic community and Russia are numerous, both in terms of values and interests, and in terms of policies. Indeed, in many ways they are fundamental. Senior Russian officials, politicians and observers have often stated their disagreements with NATO and its member states, not least their opposition to NATO enlargement and other alliance activities, and their view that NATO should be disbanded. But these are already extensively and well documented elsewhere and it is not the purpose of this book to reiterate them.

At the same time, if the calls from Bradshaw and other Western senior officials and observers for the need for a grand strategy for dealing with Russia are to be heeded,[21] then so should be the reminder from Western strategic thinkers that good strategy presumes an ability to 'read' one's adversaries and their actions. An empathetic approach highlights the features of Moscow's thinking, and serves as a reminder how different the world looks to the Russian leadership.

While the debate about international security appears – superficially – similar to the one in the Euro-Atlantic community, Moscow often draws very different conclusions from the same body of evidence – and sometimes from different bodies of evidence. There is much debate in Russia about a 'new Cold War' (or 'Cold War 2.0'), the threat posed by international terrorism and particularly Islamic fundamentalist terrorism, the war in Syria and cyber (in)security. But the premises of these debates and the thrust and detail of the arguments are often so substantially at odds with Western ones that they may appear peculiar to some Euro-Atlantic audiences. That does not mean, however, that such views are not seriously held in Moscow, or that they are not based on rational Russian thinking. Understanding these differences in detail is important for understanding Russian assumptions (and therefore strategy), and it is at least a partial antidote to the widespread problem of mirror imaging.

We will return to this theme later, but it is worth briefly illustrating some of these differences, and the strong sense of inversion or reflection of arguments. First, since Russia's annexation of Crimea, much Western attention has been paid to 'hybrid warfare' as a new form of *Russian* warfare. In Russia, however, it is understood as a *Western* form of warfare. In the article which spurred so much of this debate, Gerasimov was not so much prophesying a new form of *Russian* warfare, as ruminating on the so-called 'Arab Spring' as an example of twenty-first century warfare that is related to forced regime change and 'colour revolution' type operations. Others have emphasised the roles of 'controlled chaos' and humanitarian intervention in which the Euro-Atlantic community, led by the United States, instigate externally coordinated *coups d'état* against states that disagree with them.[22]

Russian foreign minister Lavrov illustrated this when he said that Western sanctions are a tool not just to seek to change Russian policy but to change the regime. He suggested that

> It has become fashionable to argue that Russia is waging a kind of 'hybrid war' in Crimea and Ukraine ... but I would apply it above all to the United States and its war strategy. It's truly a hybrid war aimed not so much at defeating the enemy militarily as at changing the regimes in states that pursue policy that Washington does not like.

Tools include financial and economic pressure, informational attacks, the use of proxies and informational and ideological pressure through externally financed non-governmental organisations.[23] Such views are shared across the Russian leadership and frequently and repeatedly emphasised. In spring 2016, Alexander Bastrykin, head of the Investigative Committee, called for the creation of an effective barrier against the information war, and stated that 'over the past decade Russia and a number of other countries have been living through a so-called "hybrid war", unleashed by the US and its allies. The war has been conducted on various fronts, political, economic, informational and legal'.[24]

More broadly, there is much discussion in the Russian policy community about international instability, the possibility of conflict, even the inevitability of war. This began even before the deterioration in relations between the Euro-Atlantic community and Russia in 2014. In 2013, Russian observers were suggesting that the world is in systemic crisis – economic and financial stagnation as exemplified by the global financial crisis of 2008, socio-political turbulence, even revolution as illustrated in 2011–12, and instability caused by Western humanitarian and anti-terrorist interventions and the problematic but increasing use of force to solve international problems. They argued that major geopolitical changes loomed. Such arguments have only increased since then, and a particular concern is the role of the United States in international affairs.

These points have been well illustrated by Putin himself in numerous speeches. In December 2013 he said that the world was becoming 'ever more complicated' as a fierce battle for resources was taking place and the intensity of military, political, economic and informational competition was only growing. Russia needed to be self-sufficient, with a consolidated society to face this. Moreover, he suggested that the West was 'uncompromising' with Russia, forcing Russia into a situation where Moscow had to take measures in response.[25]

The following year, in a speech that deserves to be much better known in the Euro-Atlantic community, Putin stated that 'today we are seeing new efforts to fragment the world, draw new dividing lines ... and steps of this kind inevitably create confrontation and countermeasures'. 'Today we see a sharp increase in the likelihood of a whole set of violent conflicts with either the direct or indirect participation by the world's major powers', he continued. He also suggested that 'slogans such as the "homeland is in danger", the "free world is under threat" and "democracy is in jeopardy" – so everyone needs to mobilise' reflect what a 'real mobilisation policy looks like'.[26] The Russian president appears to believe that some Euro-Atlantic states are mobilising – a point also echoed in some Russian military planning documents. It is perhaps hardly surprising, therefore, that both sides accuse each other of living in virtual realities. But that does not absolve us from attempting to grasp Moscow's reality, which is the foundation of their efforts to make strategy.

The second caveat relates to a limitation in the book's scope. Russian grand strategy and mobilisation open up a huge range of specific and complex themes, many of which are subjects worthy of detailed exploration in their own right: decision-making, corruption, Russia's economic problems, Russian military reform, Russia's ability to forge international alliances and ad hoc partnerships, and so on. Equally, there is a proliferation of Russian planning documents. The intent here is not to address all these features in depth, but to capture the main features of Russian grand strategy and set a foundation for further debate. Similarly, the intention is to illuminate an argument about broader Russian grand strategy during the Putin era, as opposed to more specific *strategies* either towards Ukraine or Syria, or the Euro-Atlantic community.

Though some – even many – of the features of Russian grand strategy will be familiar to strategists the world over, no attempt is made explicitly to compare Russian grand strategy to that of other states, nor is there an attempt to contribute to the debate about whether authoritarian states do strategy better than democratic states. Nor, for that matter, does the book reflect on the current state of Russian democracy, which has already been addressed extensively, though it is worth noting tangentially that the argument that the Russian political and security landscape is being transformed as a result of Moscow's efforts to make strategy is not to suggest any form of liberalisation. Moscow's priority is security through modernisation.

Instead, the book draws on the work of leading thinkers in the field of strategy to define grand strategy and thus reintroduce some of the core tenets of what strategy is to thinking about contemporary Russian activity. This refocuses the argument, shifting the balance of attention away from goals and towards the assumptions and processes of the formulation and implementation of plans. As the book argues, it is the vertical of power that is the heart of Russian grand strategy.

The argument also points to a longer trajectory and transition in Russia, rather than attempting to offer a direct answer to the more immediate question 'what will Putin do next?' Grasping this transition is becoming all the more important because of the increasing sense of competition between the Euro-Atlantic community and Russia, and because the Russian authorities are making progress in some areas of strategy-making.

Notes

1 'Vladimir Putin's Interview with Radio Europe 1 and TF1 TV Channel', Website of the Presidential Administration [below WPA] (4 June 2014), http://kremlin.ru/news/45832.

2 'Former Ambassador to Russia: Putin has no Master Plan for Ukraine', *NPR* (15 May 2014), www.npr.org/2014/05/15/312822551/former-ambassador-to-russia-putin-has-no-master-plan-for-ukraine; L. Freedman, *The Limits of Strategy*, Global Strategies Series (7 April 2016), www.lse.ac.uk/IDEAS/Projects/strategy/global_strategies.aspx; J. Rovner, 'Dealing with Putin's Strategic Incompetence', *War on the Rocks* (12 August 2015), https://warontherocks.com/2015/08/dealing-with-putins-strategic-incompetence/; House of Commons Foreign Affairs Committee, *The United Kingdom's Relations with Russia*. Seventh Report of Session 2016–17, HC 120 (London: HoC, March 2017), p. 23.

3 C. Wallander, 'Domestic Sources of Russia's Less-Than-Grand-Strategy', in A. Tellis and M. Wills (eds), *Strategic Asia 2007–2008: Domestic Politics, Change and Grand Strategy* (Washington, DC: National Bureau of Asian Research, 2007), p. 140.

4   For instance, Fareed Zakaria's documentary, 'The Most Powerful Man in the World', *CNN* (13 March 2017), www.youtube.com/watch?v=ImIuPKqSJNw, which features a number of prominent former officials and observers, and K. Gessen, 'Killer, Kleptocrat, Genius, Spy: The Many Myths of Vladimir Putin', *Guardian* (22 February 2017), www.theguardian.com/world/2017/feb/22/vladimir-putin-killer-genius-kleptocrat-spy-myths.

5   'NATO and EU Need a "Grand Strategy" to Resist Putin, Says General', *Financial Times* (3 March 2017).

6   *Russia: Implications for UK Defence and Security*. Report of the Defence Committee of the House of Commons, First Session 2016–17, HC 107 (5 July 2016), and the annex of the British government's response at www.publications.parliament.uk/pa/cm201617/cmselect/cmdfence/668/66804.htm. V. Gerasimov, 'Tsennost nauki v predvideniye' [The Value of Science in Foresight], *Voenno-promyshlenny Kurier* (27 February 2013), http://vpk-news.ru/articles/14632.

7   D. Schoen, *Putin's Master Plan to Destroy Europe, Divide NATO and Restore Russian Power and Global Influence* (London: Encounter Books, 2016), pp. vi–xv; M. McKew, 'Putin's Real Long Game', *Politico* (1 January 2017), www.politico.com/magazine/story/2017/01/putins-real-long-game-214589.

8   K. Sivkov, 'Strategiyu natsionalnoi bezopasnosti razrabativali dvoechniki', *Voenno-Promyshlenny Kurier* (11 December 2013).

9   R. Pukhov, 'The World Vs. Russia' (15 August 2013), www.forceindia.net/TheWorldvsRussia.aspx.

10   M. Zygar, *Vsya Kremlyovskaya rat'. Kratkaya istoriya sovremennoi Rossii* (Moscow: Intellektualnaya literatura, 2016), p. 6.

11   M. Delyagin *et al.*, *Strategiya 'bolshovo ryvka'* (Moscow: Algorythm, 2012). 'Bolshovo ryvka' is ambiguous in English, and could also be rendered as a 'big push' strategy – but still, the emphasis of the project remains on mobilisation.

12   'Zasedanie mezhdurarodnovo diskussionnovo kluba "Valdai"', WPA (19 September 2013), http://kremlin.ru/events/president/news/19243.

13   'Poslaniye Prezidenta federalnomu sobraniyu', WPA (12 December 2013), www.kremlin.ru/transcripts/19825; 'Rasshirennoe zasedanie Pravitelstva', WPA (31 January 2013), http://kremlin.ru/events/president/news/17396.

14   For more on 'Putinology', see A. Monaghan, *The New Politics of Russia: Interpreting Change* (Manchester: Manchester University Press, 2016).

15   C. Gray, *The Future of Strategy* (Cambridge: Polity, 2015), pp. 31, 109.

16   Ibid., pp. 83, 86.

17   Freedman, *The Limits of Strategy*; also H. Brands, *What Good is Grand Strategy? Power and Purpose in American Statecraft From Harry S. Truman to George W. Bush* (London: Cornell University Press, 2014).

18   M. Dudziak, *War Time: An Idea, its History, its Consequences* (Oxford: Oxford University Press, 2012), pp. 131, 134.

19   'Peskov: Reaktsiya rukovodstva Turtsii na intsident Su-24 napominaet teatr absurda', *Tass News* (28 November 2015), http://tass.ru/politika/2481443.

20   For definitions, see the websites of the Russian Ministry of Defence (http://encyclopedia.mil.ru/encyclopedia/dictionary.htm) and Ministry of Emergencies (www.mchs.gov.ru/dop/terms/item/86320).

21   P. Breedlove, 'NATO's Next Act', *Foreign Affairs* (July/August 2016); A. Jain *et al.*, *Strategy of Constrainment. Countering Russia's Challenge to the Democratic Order* (Washington, DC: Atlantic Council, March 2017).

22   For the best English language analysis of this article by Gerasimov, see C. Bartles, 'Getting Gerasimov Right', *Military-Review* (January–February 2016), http://fmso.leavenworth.army.mil/Regional%20security%20europe/MilitaryReview_20160228_art009.pdf. For a Russian critique, see R. Pukhov, 'Mif o gibridnoi voine', *Nezavisimaya Gazeta* (29 May 2015), http://nvo.ng.ru/realty/2015–05–29/1_war.html, and for Russian thinking on 'controlled chaos' and the 'colour revolutions', V. Karyakin,

Geopolitika tretei volny: transformatsiya mira v epokhu Postmoderna (Moscow: Granitsa, 2013).

23   Remarks by Foreign Minister Sergey Lavrov at the XXII Assembly of the Council on Foreign and Defence Policy, Moscow, Website of the Russian Embassy in London (22 November 2014), www.rusemb.org.uk/video/231.

24   A. Bastrykin, 'Pora postavit deistvennyi zaslon informatsionnoi voine', *Kommersant* (18 April 2016), http://kommersant.ru/doc/2961578. Russian officials frequently point to cyber attacks on Russia both on financial institutions and on elections.

25   'Poslaniye Prezidenta Federalnomu Sobraniyu', WPA (12 December 2013), http://kremlin.ru/events/president/news/19825.

26   'Zasedaniye mezhdunarodnovo kluba "Valdai"', WPA (24 October 2014), http://kremlin.ru/events/president/news/46860.

1

Setting a strategic agenda

UNDER Vladimir Putin, the Russian leadership has consistently sought to shape a strategic agenda. In December 1999, when prime minister and acting president, Putin published a 'millennium' article outlining his views on the situation in Russia. He wrote about the lessons to be learnt from Russia's history, the crisis Russia faced and possible opportunities. He identified a strong state and efficient economy as the keys to its recovery, and what Russia needed, he suggested, was to 'formulate a long-term strategy', one that would help to overcome the crisis.[1] Subsequently, the Russian leadership has often reiterated this commitment in a series of major planning documents, supplemented by articles by senior figures, and prominent speeches such as the president's annual speech to the Federal Assembly.

This strategic planning process is multifaceted and more complex than allowed for in most discussions of Russian strategy. It opens up three sets of questions that are central to our understanding of the 'formulation' aspects of Russian grand strategy. These are, first, the strategy planning process and the legislative and policy architecture that has taken shape; second, the nature of the agenda itself, partly as framed in the documents relating to foreign and security policy, but more particularly Putin's May Edicts of 2012, which set out Moscow's core strategic agenda; and third, the questions raised by the numerous problems in planning and the extent to which they undermine the idea of Russian grand strategy, even at the stage of its formulation.

Shaping a planning process

Since the mid-2000s, the commitment to strategic planning has become codified in legislation. Indeed, the need for a more systematic approach to it emerged at a meeting of the State Council in mid-2006 at which it became clear that there was no legal basis for a comprehensive federal level strategy. What turned out to be a lengthy and rather complex process was launched to establish just such a basis. This led first to the order 'On the Foundations of Strategic Planning' (2009), which framed strategic planning as the determination of the directions and the means of achieving the strategic goals of the stable development of Russia and providing for national security, and then the 'Law on Strategic Planning'.[2]

One of Russia's most prominent strategic thinkers, Andrei Kokoshin, wrote in 2007 that the 'application of strategic planning means a significantly higher level of governance than governance based on reacting to immediate situations'. Putin's directive to create a state system of strategic planning, he suggested, was fully justified as one of the mechanisms for a strategy for Russia's development. 'The advancing of this kind of strategy has a political-mobilisation function', he said.[3]

The order on the Foundations of Strategic Planning set out the legal basis for the preparation, development and function of the system of strategic planning in the areas of socio-economic development and national security, and set out both a time-frame for strategic planning in stages and an understanding of a process of foresight and response to developments likely to impinge on Russian society. It also provides for the introduction of mechanisms for the monitoring and control of the implementation of documents. It covers state, regional and municipal governance and the coordination of the respective organs of power, including the presidential executive, government, both Houses of Parliament, and the Central Bank.

A number of organisations are involved in contributing to strategic planning. The relevant ministries are responsible for planning in their own sector, but the Ministry for Economic Development has been tasked not only with elaborating economic plans but also drafting the law on strategic planning. The Russian Academy of Sciences and Higher School of Economics have contributed to planning and preparation the documents, as have a number of think tanks.

Perhaps most notable, though, is the role of the Security Council (SC). In 2006, the SC formed an inter-agency commission dedicated to strategic planning, and began to play an increasingly important role in the process. Indeed, since then, and particularly since Nikolai Patrushev was appointed secretary in 2008,[4] it has emerged as the dominant feature of this process, the main reservoir of ministerial resources and authority. The core of the SC consists of a permanent membership drawn from the security and law enforcement services and parliament which meets regularly.[5]

The Council has taken on the central role in the overhaul of the documentation that began in 2006, and become the main organ for forging consensus and coordinating strategic planning, and the preparation of the various strategies, concepts, doctrines and programmes. Its role has been incrementally strengthened by legislation – not just that on strategic planning, but also by presidential orders, which have reinforced its powers so that they go beyond forecasting and threat assessment towards a greater role in formulating and implementing policy. According to a presidential decree of 2011, it 'forms the main directions of state domestic and foreign policy',[6] and in 2013, Patrushev stated that it had become the chief inter-agency coordinator of decisions on the main tasks in domestic and foreign policy, both formulating policy and overseeing its implementation.[7] The SC's remit is broadly defined as a national security agenda, including the security of the state and society, socio-economic security and information security, as well as defence and international affairs.

Shaping a strategic agenda

The timing of the decision to create a more systematic strategic planning process was significant because of the difficult context Moscow then faced. Domestically, not only had there been major terrorist attacks in Russia but major social reforms had failed, leading to large protest demonstrations in 2005. The international context was no less demanding, given the 'colour revolutions' in Georgia and Ukraine and a sharply deteriorating relationship with the Euro-Atlantic community as a result of disagreements over international developments such as the Iraq war and also in the bilateral relationship with growing Western criticism of Russian governance.[8] Existing Russian strategic plans, including 'Strategy 2010', no longer corresponded to this challenging context and required updating.

Thus, alongside the structural process the leadership conducted an overhaul of the main strategic planning processes and agenda, one which led to the publication between 2008 and 2010 of a cascade of updated strategic outlook documents. These took the form of a series of strategies, concepts and doctrines, and included the National Security Strategy of the Russian Federation to 2020 (2009), the Long-term Socio-economic Development Plan to 2020 (2008), and updated versions of the Foreign Policy Concept (2008) and Military Doctrine (2010). These were supplemented by Medvedev's article 'Russia Forward!' (2009) and initiatives in foreign policy, such as the proposals for a new European security treaty (2008).

These documents illustrated the main assumptions about Russia and its place in international affairs. The main themes were that Russia was in the process of resolving – or had already resolved – many of the problems it had faced in the 1990s and that its main goal was to become a leading state on the international stage by preserving its independence and influence as a sovereign actor, particularly in the Eurasian region. To do so, a dual focus was necessary – to invest in infrastructure and economic modernisation in Russia, and to build regional integration so that Russia would become a hub in the Eurasian region through the promotion of projects such as the Customs Union, the Eurasian Economic Union and the Collective Security Treaty Organisation.

Another stage began in 2011–12, with the return of economic growth, and efforts to consolidate strategic planning further and continue to update plans. Many of the assumptions and aims in this third stage remained consistent. During his speech to the Federal Assembly in 2012, for instance, Putin emphasised the sense of continuity, stating that national reconstruction and strengthening had been completed and that the task was to build a rich and prosperous Russia that could retain its sovereignty and influence in a competitive world marked by an increasing sense of conflict. Russia, he said, had to preserve its geopolitical relevance and even increase it.

This stage began with the preparation of an informal 'Strategy 2020' document, commissioned by Putin in January 2011 and published in March 2012. This project brought together some 1,500 specialists in twenty-one working groups to offer a range of scenarios and policy options.[9] But it is best understood as having two main pillars. The first represents the core strategic agenda, and is in the shape of the so-called May Edicts of 2012, a set of eleven presidential Edicts signed into force by Putin on his return to the Kremlin in May 2012. They expanded on a series of articles he had published during his election campaign, and he has frequently emphasised ever since that they are the central plank of Russia's strategic agenda.

The Edicts cover a vast, and in many ways aspirational, agenda, one that includes economic and social policy, healthcare, housing and utilities, education and science, inter-ethnic relations, demography, state administration, as well as foreign policy (including foreign economic relations) and military matters. Each Edict gives a sweep from the very broadest level, such as the need to prepare updated legislation, to the very specific. The overall thrust is the attempt to modernise Russia, to drag it into the twenty-first century, by restoring economic dynamism, improving living conditions, for instance by building at least 25 million square metres of new housing with social infrastructure, and modernising and expanding Russian military power.

This latter point was framed in two of the Edicts: one on improvements to military service conditions, including improvement of pensions and other conditions, and the intention yearly to recruit tens of thousands of contract troops, the other on modernising the military industrial complex and the armed forces. This included priority focus on increasing the share of modern arms and technology to the armed forces and other organs to 70 per cent by 2020, the priority development of Russia's strategic nuclear deterrent and other capabilities.[10]

Putin has emphasised that this modernisation process predates the escalating emergency since 2014, and is intended to make good the chronic underfunding for the armed forces and defence industry in the post-Cold War era. He has also stated that it is necessary because other leading states are investing in modernising their armed forces, including developing strategic projection and high-precision conventional capabilities. It also has wider ramifications. As Putin has noted, the defence industry plays a crucial role in social stability, particularly during the economic downturn, because it employs hundreds of thousands of people.[11] Putin has also suggested that the development of the defence companies has an important socio-economic role, since the defence industry represents some 3 per cent of Russia's total employment and dominates the economies of a number of cities and regions. It thus contributes to maintaining social stability.

Alongside this was the second pillar, the ongoing updating of the main strategic documents, such as the Foreign Policy Concept (2013 and again in 2016), Military Doctrine (2014) and the National Security Strategy (2015) and either the long-overdue updating of, or the introduction of, a plethora of new strategies, concepts and doctrines dealing with a wide range of subjects from maritime affairs to food security, from a state anti-drugs policy strategy to 2020 to anti-terrorist strategies and from information security to the Arctic.

It also included important but often overlooked developments. The first of these was the refreshment of legislation dealing with mobilisation of the economy, a process which appears to have begun in December 2008. In 2010, Putin signed off a concept for the improvement of mobilisation preparation of the economy, and in 2011 he approved a decision to prepare a new mobilisation plan for the economy to be ready for 2014. According to Julian Cooper, this document reflects a fundamental break with the Soviet past and the 1990s in the way that it shifted the mobilisation away from the conservation of production capacities. The move towards the sharp increase in production of military goods and only focusing on armaments specified in the current arms programme and thus already in volume production, he argues, is similar to the surge capability of the United States and other NATO states.[12]

A significant addition to strategic planning during this period was the Defence Plan. Initially presented by Defence Minister Sergei Shoigu and Gerasimov to Putin in January 2013, the Defence Plan has received only limited attention in Western commentary to date, but it appears to be a central document, and Patrushev has suggested that it is a 'principally new element' in Russian planning. It is a complex of interconnected strategic and operational documents to forecast 'developments in the military and political situation. It also formulates a unified defence policy that includes military, economic, information and other aspects and sets out the main tasks for strategic deterrence, preventing military conflicts from arising and resolving the main mobilization tasks'. With an emphasis on coordination of forty-nine Russian ministries and agencies, it appears to be both closely related to the newly opened National Defence Management Centre, of which more in Chapter 4, and a 'live' working document, being regularly updated and clarified. In November 2015, Putin signed a newly updated version for 2016–20, but noted that since the international situation was quickly changing the Defence Ministry should work with other departments and submit 'clarifications and adjustments'.[13]

This returns us to Moscow's assumptions. As noted in the Introduction, the Russian policy debate among officials and observers alike reflects a pessimistic set of assumptions that are often different to those of the Euro-Atlantic community. Many in Russia see international affairs as having entered a transitional period, a long-term evolution accelerated by the global financial crisis and exacerbated by the activities of leading Western states in which instability and conflict will persist throughout the 2020s. The main features of this are the European Union's financial and economic and migration crises, socio-political turbulence in North Africa and the Middle East and the concurrent decline of the Western, and particularly the Anglo-Saxon, powers and the rise of other states and regions. In January 2012, in one of his campaign articles that formed the basis for the May Edicts, Putin stated that the world faces 'serious systemic crisis' and is entering a 'zone of turbulence which will be long and painful',[14] and these pessimistic assumptions about turbulence and competition permeate Moscow's strategic planning documents.

Concerns broadly fall into two categories. First, for much of the last decade, there has been concern about what Moscow perceives to be modern Western ways of war – as discussed in the Introduction, war using hybrid methods to achieve regime change. This is seen to pose a threat to wider regional stability, for instance in Iraq, Libya and Syria, to stability on Russia's borders, as illustrated by Ukraine, and even directly to Russia. These concerns have their roots in the so-called 'colour revolutions' in Georgia, Ukraine and Kyrgyzstan from 2003 to 2005. Senior Russian officials have often pointed to their concerns about colour revolutions as a means of achieving regime change, and asserted that the protest demonstrations in Russia in 2011 were supported by the United States to this same end. Putin has pointed to the need to learn lessons from colour revolutions, asserting that every effort must be made to prevent one from happening in Russia. In March 2015, he said that he saw 'attempts to use so-called colour revolution technology ranging from organizing unlawful protests to open propaganda of hatred and enmity in social networks'. The aim was obvious, he suggested: to 'strike a blow at [Russia's] sovereignty'.[15]

The Russian authorities link such concerns to questions of terrorism. On one hand, they state that extremism is used as one of the tools of regime change: financial, political and informational support for terrorists is used to undermine and attack states, including Russia itself. On the other, they argue that the result of regime change operations is the eruption of chaos and instability, conditions in which terrorism thrives, as illustrated by Libya and Syria. Concern about colour revolution is often related, therefore, to concern about international terrorism and groups, essentially, according to Putin, 'terrorist armies' that receive 'tacit and sometimes even open support from some countries', take active part in conflicts in the Middle East, Asia and Africa.[16]

The second set of concerns relates more to the possible eruption of conflict and war. As noted in the Introduction, in 2014 Putin suggested that Moscow saw a 'sharp increase in the likelihood of a whole set of violent conflicts with either the direct or indirect participation by the world's powers'. Indeed, the lessons of history indicated that such great changes in the international architecture have 'usually been accompanied if not by global war and conflict, then by chains of intensive low-level conflicts', he continued. A year later, he pointed to a widespread 'deficit of security' across many regions of the world, which, combined with the increasing intensity of military, economic, political and informational competition, meant that the 'potential for conflict in the world is growing, old contradictions are growing ever more acute and new ones are being provoked'.[17]

The main points underpinning this view are concerns about competition for resources and influence at a time of increasing of strategic instability caused by an arms race. 'Most of the world's leading countries are actively upgrading their military arsenals and investing huge sums in developing advanced weapons systems', Putin stated in December 2013, which was leading to a situation in which there are attempts 'to violate and disturb the strategic balance'.[18]

Earlier that year, Gerasimov had also argued that Russia may be drawn into military conflicts as states compete for resources, many of which are in Russia or its neighbourhood. By 2030, he stated, 'the level of existing and potential threats will significantly increase' as powers struggle for fuel, energy and labour resources, as well as new markets in which to sell their goods. In his February 2013 article, he also pointed to the US Prompt Global Strike programme and its missile defence programme, both of which 'foresee the defeat of enemy objects and forces in a matter of hours from almost any point on the globe, while at the same time ensuring the prevention of unacceptable harm from an enemy counterstrike'.[19]

Planning problems

Despite the broad creation of a strategic planning architecture and a proliferation of documents, there are a series of ongoing problems with both process and documents. These can be divided into three main groups that produce a set of complex difficulties for Moscow's attempts to form a strategic agenda. First, as discussed in the Introduction, there are inherent difficulties in strategic planning. It requires attempting foresight despite the obvious uncertainty of attempting to look into a 'foggy' future, and regardless of how well it is done, the friction of events will require plans to be updated. Russian strategic planning has not escaped these difficulties.

The global economic crisis of 2008 meant that large parts of 2008's Long-term Socio-Economic Development Concept were immediately rendered obsolete and programmes were stopped even before they had begun. The May Edicts, too, faced serious opposition from events: the intention to improve economic relations with the United States was stalled almost immediately by the outbreak of war in Ukraine and the sanctions. Furthermore, they were signed into force with the expectation of 4–5 per cent GDP growth. But almost immediately, the Russian economy began a prolonged decline into stagnation and then recession,[20] with implications that will be discussed in Chapter 2.

Foreign and security policy planning also suffered from this opposition of events. For Moscow, as for most others, the revolutions in North Africa and the Middle East came as a surprise, and dated the Foreign Policy Concept of 2008. One of the May Edicts included the instruction to update the Foreign Policy Concept by the end of 2012, which was duly done, with the new document published in early 2013. A year later, however, the war in Ukraine erupted and the situation in Syria deteriorated severely, effectively rendering even the new concept so dated that a further update was commissioned ahead of schedule to take into account these new circumstances.

Uncertainty has also caused delays, particularly in budget preparation and energy sector planning. The prolonged delay in producing the Energy Strategy to 2035, for instance, was partly due to the ongoing questions about so many of the basic planning assumptions and the serious implications of getting them wrong.[21]

The other problems relate more specifically to the Russian political and planning landscape. It is a commonplace that Vladimir Putin is the driving force behind Russian strategic planning. But if this is in many ways true it is not the whole picture, and the wider bureaucratic landscape and structure play important roles. As we shall see again in Chapter 2, not everyone in Russia follows the script. The second problem, therefore, is that strategic planning in Moscow is not monolithic, and numerous disagreements have beset not just the plans, but also the process.

The draft law on strategic planning illustrates this well. The Ministry of Economic Development presented an initial draft in 2008 which emphasised socio-economic development but largely ignored national security questions. The government returned the draft for further work, apparently following criticism from the Ministry of Finance. A second version was submitted in November 2011 but again faced objections from the Ministry of Finance (on the grounds that the approach to strategic planning was not sufficiently coordinated with budget planning and opening the possibility that commitments might be made in planning that would subsequently threaten macroeconomic stability) and the Security Council.

Julian Cooper has suggested that the Security Council's objections came from two sources – the division of strategic planning into separate socio-economic and national security spheres, which would conflict with other strategic planning legislation, and that it had not been involved in the drafting of the plan. Another version was submitted to the Duma, which again imposed revisions before the law came into force – finally – in 2014, eight years after it was commissioned by Putin.[22]

Third, there are a number of bureaucratic problems that affect the formulation of the plans. Russian observers, for instance, have criticised the 'galloping deprofessionalisation' of the Russian bureaucracy, and asserted that the National Security Strategy had been prepared by 'dunces',[23] and others criticised a cavalier approach to the preparation of plans, even suggesting that supportive statistics had been simply fabricated.

Furthermore, the leadership's emphasis on strategic planning has placed a huge burden on what is a rather limited bureaucratic apparatus. Ministries are required to prepare a very large number of documents, from strategic concepts to plans for regional development. This in itself does not necessarily prevent strategic planning, but it limits the ability to develop initiatives concurrently and in the detail that makes the plans implementable. Indeed, the leadership often admonishes the bureaucracy for producing vaguely worded documents. Putin has, for instance, criticised ministries – including in security and law enforcement – for producing documents that neither provide guidelines for action, nor concrete objectives, nor indicate priority working areas, but only contain language such as 'engage' and 'enhance'. The plans are thus returned to the ministries for further work under Putin and Medvedev's direct control. Even when a document is adopted, departmental action and legislation on specific progress are not developed, and so no practical progress is made implementing them.[24]

These difficulties introduce a range of problems with the documents. Though they are broadly coherent, there are some noteworthy contradictions, such as those in the law on strategic planning, as well as inconsistencies and gaps. Strategy 2020 planning did not address issues such as Russia's accession to the World Trade Organization, the challenges facing the agricultural sector, which had been identified by Putin as a priority, and nor did it address the sensitive question of whether economic reform could be achieved without political reform. Inconsistency in economic and energy planning has contributed to delays in energy planning as the Energy Ministry sought to meet ambitious import substitution targets. And there are noteworthy omissions in foreign and security policy: in the Military Doctrine of 2010, for instance, little attention was given to the major reforms of the armed forces that were under way at the time of its publication. This reflected, according to one astute Russian commentator, ongoing indecision between departments, shifting goalposts mid-reform, and reversals of reforms already underway.[25] China, often said by the leadership to be a major priority for Russian foreign policy, was, until the most recent editions of the Foreign Policy Concept and National Security Strategy, largely neglected in the formal documents, let alone the subject of clear strategic planning.

Russian strategic planning is flawed, therefore, both in terms of achieving consensus, and in balancing the political flexibility necessary to achieve consensus with the precision needed for those who implement the plans. Many of these flaws − not least the difficulties of forecasting and achieving consensus across agencies and ministries − will be familiar to strategy-makers everywhere.

Nevertheless, over the last decade or so, a broadly structured strategic planning process has emerged, both in legislation and institutions such as the Security Council. This provides the basis from which the Russian leadership seeks to formulate plans. True, the documents themselves are susceptible to being rendered out of date, sometimes quite quickly, by events. This by itself does not mean that the plans are 'unstrategic', however, given the regular refreshments and updates that are now part of the structured planning process.

And while the documents are often formulaic, if read carefully, they illustrate that the Russian leadership thinks strategically and has set out a strategic agenda. The core of this agenda is in the May Edicts, which provide the guiding purpose. Related to this is the cascade of other planning documents, which, together with speeches and other initiatives, set out the basic approaches of the Russian leadership. If they are sometimes short on specific policy prescriptions even for priority areas, they serve to illuminate Moscow's broadly consistent, albeit pessimistic, strategic assumptions.

Notes

1   V. Putin, 'Rossiya na rubezhe tisyacheletii', *Nezavisimaya Gazeta* (30 December 1999), www.ng.ru/politics/1999–12–30/4_millenium.html. A short document entitled 'The Strategy of Development of the Russian Federation to 2010' ensued.

2   J. Cooper, 'Reviewing Russian Strategic Planning: The Emergence of Strategy 2020', *Russian Studies Series*, NATO Defence College (June 2012) offers a thorough review of this process.

3   A. Kokoshin, *O strategicheskom planirovanii v politike* (Moscow: URSS, 2007), pp. 8–10.

4   Patrushev is a long-term, close ally of Putin. Prior to his appointment as Secretary of the Security Council, he served as Director of the Federal Security Service (FSB) from 1999 to 2008.

5   Only Dmitri Medvedev in his position as prime minister might be said to represent the socio-economic agenda in the SC's permanent membership, though he is not an economist. Though Finance Minister Anton Siluanov is a member of the wider second tier, even in this wider group the economic sector is poorly represented.

6   'On Matters Concerning the Security Council of the Russian Federation', Presidential Edict no. 590, 6 May 2011. The author is grateful to Keir Giles for this point.

7   'Meeting with the Permanent Members of the Security Council', WPA (11 December 2013), http://news.kremlin.ru/news/19823; Patrushev interviewed in *Rossiiskaya Gazeta* (27 December 2013).

8   For discussion of these protests and also the deterioration of the relationship between Russia and the Euro-Atlantic community, see Monaghan, *The New Politics of Russia*.

9 Strategy 2020 was beset by a number of problems. It was limited to economic matters and the structure of the project was such that it was badly coordinated. The result was a bulky 864-page document that failed to offer a coherent vision and, in the words of one experienced Russian observer, 'lay unopened on the table'.

10 The two Edicts are 'O dalneishem sovershenstvovanii voennoi sluzhby v Rossiiskoi Federatsii', Edict no. 604, 7 May 2012, and 'O realizatsii planov {program} stroitelstva i razvitiya Vooruzhonnikh Sil Rossiskoi Federatsii drugikh voisk, voinskikh formirovanii i organov i modernizatsii oboronno-promyshlennovo kompleksa', Edict no. 603, May 2012. In February 2013, Putin stated that this should be 30 per cent by 2015 and 70–100 per cent by 2020, and that these weapons should be produced by Russian defence companies, 'Rasshirennoe zasedaniye kollegii Ministerstva oborony', 2013.

11 'Soveshchanie po voprosam razvitiya Vooruzhonnykh Sil', WPA (9 November 2015), http://kremlin.ru/events/president/news/50648.

12 For more detailed discussion, see J. Cooper, *If War Comes Tomorrow: How Russia Prepares for Possible Armed Aggression.* Whitehall Report 4–16 (London: RUSI, August 2016), pp. 18–23.

13 'Rasshinennoe zasedaniye kollegii Ministerstva oborony', WPA (27 February 2013), http://kremlin.ru/events/president/news/17588; 'Rasshirennoe zasedaniye kollegii Ministerstva oborony', WPA (11 December 2015), http://kremlin.ru/events/president/news/50913. The title of the document is slightly ambiguous: in Russian, it is titled the Defence Plan ('plan oborony'), but the official translation is 'Defence Strategy', http://kremlin.ru/events/president/news/17385; 'FSB raskinet set', *Rossiiskaya Gazeta* (20 February 2013), www.scrf.gov.ru/news/allnews/766/.

14 V. Putin, 'Rossiya sosredatochivaetsa – vyzovy, na kotorie my dolzhny otvetit', *Izvestia* (16 January 2012).

15 'Rasshirennoe zasedaniye kollegii MVD', WPA (4 March 2015), http://kremlin.ru/events/president/news/47776.

16 'Zasedaniye kollegii Federalnoi sluzhby bezopasnosti', WPA (16 February 2017), http://kremlin.ru/events/president/news/53883.

17 'Soveshaniye poslov i postoyannykh predstavitelei Rossii', WPA (1 July 2015), http://kremlin.ru/events/president/news/46131.

18 'Rasshirenoe zasedanie kollegii Minoborony', WPA (10 December 2013), http://kremlin.ru/events/president/news/19816.

19 'Russia may be Drawn into Resource Wars in Future – Army Chief', *Russia Today* (14 February 2013); Gerasimov, 'Tsennost nauki'.

20 The economic decline became particularly steep in late 2013, and accelerated in 2014 as a result of the blend of the sharp decline in oil prices, capital outflow and the sanctions. It took until late 2017 before any signs of recovery began to show.

21 N. Mehdiyeva, 'When Sanctions Bite: Global Export Leadership in a Competitive World and the Russian Energy Strategy to 2035', *Russian Studies* 01/17 (Rome: NATO Defence College, January 2017), p. 3.

22 Cooper, 'Reviewing Russian Strategic Planning', pp. 7–8. Even so, full implementation has been postponed until 2019.

23 V. Inozemtsev, 'Neo-Feudalism Explained', *American Interest*, Vol. 6, No. 4 (March–April 2011); Sivkov, 'Strategiyu natsionalnoi bezopasnosti razrabativali dvoechniki'.

24 'Prezidentu predstavleny plany raboty ministerstv po ispolneniyu maiskikh ukazov', WPA (7 June 2013), www.kremlin.ru/news/18277; 'Soveshaniye o planakh deyatelnosti ministerstv napravlennoi na dostizhenie tselevykh pokazatelei sotsialnoekonomicheskovo razvitiya, opredelyonnykh prezidentom', WPA (10 June 2013), www.kremlin.ru/news/18310.

25 M. Barabanov (ed.), *Russia's New Army* (Moscow: Centre for Analysis of Strategies and Technologies, 2011); K. Giles, 'The Military Doctrine of the Russian Federation 2010', *Russian Studies* (Rome: NATO Defence College, 2010).

2

The problems of power in Russia

S TRATEGY, though, is combination of plans *and their imple-mentation*, the executive management of a purposeful set of ideas. And here too Moscow has long faced a series of important problems. Indeed, the primary difficulty for the Russian leader-ship – as for every other strategist – is that strategy is not made in a vacuum, and a series of external and domestic influences greatly complicate Russian strategy-making.

The evolving external context poses numerous difficulties for Moscow's plans. There are longer-term questions that affect the economic underpinnings of the leadership's plans: the glo-bal economic and financial crisis of 2008, for instance, had a very significant negative effect on the Russian economy – and exerted considerable subsequent influence on the leadership's thinking, which including measures to enhance the economy's resilience and the reconsideration of economic mobilisation measures noted above.

And, as Richard Connolly has noted, even as the economy began – slowly – to recover from that crisis, two other important external influences have constrained Russian economic growth. On one hand, he says, the 'most obvious external cause of the economic slowdown in Russia has been the prolonged stagna-tion in the economies of Europe, collectively Russia's largest trading partner and source of capital'. On the other, Russia has been negatively affected by the strengthening of the US dollar as the consequence of the tapering of monetary expansion in the United States. This, he suggests, intensified both capital outflows from low- and middle-income countries to the United States, and the depreciation of many currencies against the dollar and a decline in the price of oil. Thus 'while Russia is not alone in being buffeted by global headwinds, it has suffered to a greater extent than most'.[1]

Similarly, crises have had a major impact on the foundations of Russian policies. There has been much debate about whether Russia had planned the annexation of Crimea in February and March 2014, and the emergency certainly fit into the Russian leadership's understanding of the international situation. But two points suggest that Moscow did not appear to envisage such a crisis in the planning of the May Edicts. First, it resulted in the negation of one of the May Edicts' foreign policy priorities, improved economic relations with the United States. Instead, the economic and financial sanctions that the Euro-Atlantic community subsequently imposed on Russia (and those that Moscow imposed in reply) reflected the start of what was tantamount to an economic war.

Second, it resulted in restrictions on technological imports and foreign investment, particularly on dual-use technology, creating significant obstacles to military modernisation plans. The Russian defence industry was heavily reliant on foreign electronic components and engines for helicopters and power units for ships made in Ukraine. The sanctions and cutting of ties with the Ukrainian defence industry meant, therefore, that part of the modernisation of the armed forces – another May Edicts priority – suffered delays. One prominent observer of the Russian defence industry pointed out that there could be 'no quick fix for the business ties lost in Ukraine', and Russian officials specialists acknowledged delays of several years.[2] The pursuit of interests as Moscow saw them in Ukraine in 2014, therefore, in this case did little to further the central strategic agenda of the May Edicts.

The domestic context with which the Russian leadership has to deal also poses numerous obstacles to generating strategy. As Putin has said, 'of course we are feeling the effects of the global economic crisis, but let's be frank: the main reasons for the slowdown in our economy are internal rather than external in nature'.[3] There are numerous well-known problems with the Russian economy, including weak property rights, a poorly functioning financial system, a wider demographic problem that is leading to a shrinking labour force, and a lack of diversity and efficiency; and many have argued convincingly that the current leadership failed to address these problems during the 2000s when oil prices were high.

At the same time, the inheritance from the Soviet era poses a set of serious hurdles for would-be Russian strategists. The Soviet legacy continues to distort and weigh on the Russian economy, both as a result of the inherited production structure, including the types of physical and human capital, the way in which resources were allocated, and because of pricing decisions which led to overvaluation of assets and an underestimation of the rate of return on them. Poor location choices and poor use of assets are endemic in Russia, and 'bad institutions sustain the misallocations'.[4]

Furthermore, chronic underinvestment over many years has left a legacy of limited and increasingly decrepit national infrastructure. Russia's geography and climate pose serious obstacles – while Russia has (in statistical terms) a comparatively large road and rail network, large parts of the country are poorly served, if at all, by transport infrastructure. The lack of roads and the serious problems in the domestic air transport network mean that there is a heavy reliance on waterways and rail transport, but there are severe infrastructural bottlenecks in both of these systems.[5] Putin noted in 2016, for example, that through shipping on the Volga and Lower Don had come to a halt, and elsewhere freight volumes have substantially fallen. Sergei Ivanov, special presidential representative for transport, was also explicit about the scale of the problem:

> very serious infrastructure limitations for the development of the economy exist in Russia ... good roads have started to appear here, but they are almost all federal, trillions of rubles have been invested in them ... but the regional

and municipal road networks are awful. They do not have enough funds ... we will never have the money for a completely free road network.[6]

Similarly, prolonged underinvestment has meant that the rail network suffers from a lack of lines, as well as aging and obsolete rolling stock. Addressing this – modernising or, in many areas, building the necessary infrastructure – will take a long time and cost many billions of rubles: in shaping its modernisation strategy to 2030, the state-owned railway monopoly estimated that at least US$353 billion would need to be invested.[7]

Prolonged underinvestment in the housing and utilities, industry and energy sectors has resulted in deepening obsolescence and decrepitude, and power plants and industrial equipment from the mid-twentieth century remain in service.[8] Similarly, the military endured severe cuts during the 1990s, a time of deep economic crisis in Russia, resulting again in growing obsolescence and, over time, a concomitantly severe degradation in capability. As Mikhail Barabanov has put it, by 2008 the Russian military machine had become 'archaic and ineffective ... increasingly ill-suited to Russia's new political-military objectives'.[9] And, as in the housing and utilities and energy sectors, advancing decrepitude has led to a number of accidents.

While it is rare that a leadership is able to attempt to make strategy in ideal circumstances, from a blank sheet, as it were, Moscow has been attempting to do so in a particularly difficult context – with many of the tools of power decrepit and limited in capacity. Moreover, a wide range of other problems constrain and undermine Russian strategy-making. These can be broadly divided into two categories: the effective balancing of resources and the 'conducting of the orchestra'.

Coordinating resources

The May Edicts set out an ambitious agenda – effectively to drag Russia into the twenty-first century, and the cost of this agenda is correspondingly large. The targets demand a significant increase in spending and the scale of the resources required is enormous: by way of illustration, housing and utilities alone required some US$280 billion, and the military some US$680 billion.[10] Even in the context of, at the time, high oil prices and the large Russian financial resources (a huge foreign exchange reserve of nearly US$450 billion in 2011), the scale of funds required to implement the agenda was vast and required careful prioritisation and coordination to match resources to targets.

But a number of internal Russian problems exacerbated these tensions. The May Edicts, for instance, were based on a projected GDP growth of 4–5 per cent. But Russian GDP growth began a serious decline in 2011, one which accelerated in 2012–13 and on through the emergency in Ukraine, the steep fall in oil prices in 2014 and the deterioration in relations with the Euro-Atlantic community. Reduced tax proceeds, capital flight and decreasing revenues from hydrocarbon export resulted in a serious decline in revenues. A number of authorities publicly stated that they did not have the funds to implement the Edicts. In 2013, Alexei Ulyukaev, then Minister of Economic Development, suggested that the slowing growth meant that the budget would not have enough to fund the May Edicts. Anton Siluanov, the Minister of Finance, agreed, and the Finance Ministry reported that the budget lacked US$285 billion to implement the Edicts by 2020. The Audit Chamber agreed, suggesting that the regions' budgets had little more than half the required funding.[11]

Indeed, the May Edicts have put considerable pressure on regional budgets that cannot afford to finance the programmes and as a result many regions depend on federal subsidies to meet their obligations. Putin has recognised the problem with the self-sustainability of the regions, but has reiterated that regional leaders implement the Edicts regardless of the problems. 'We know the situation with regional finances. And the Finance Ministry should respond to it accordingly', he stated in spring 2014, 'but the Edicts must be implemented. I want the regional leaders, the senators representing their interests to take it as a premise'.[12]

This problem was compounded by others, most notably inefficiency in state expenditure and corruption. The extent of the inefficiency of state expenditure was acknowledged by Putin himself in 2013. Speaking at a meeting of the State Council, he emphasised that 'we have repeated again and again that the budgets are executed in a chaotic and very uneven fashion ... that some targeted programmes and planned activities are not being carried out at all ... and many budget items are unclear and amorphous'. He pointed to two sets of problems: the spreading of resources too thinly created a situation in which projects that should take only a couple of years turn into never-ending projects that go on for years, and financial indiscipline.

Indeed, Putin illuminated the systemic nature of the latter problem, stating that budget law was often 'blatantly ignored': in 2012 cases of violating budget laws cost 187 billion rubles, and clarifying that this was not theft or corruption but a lack of proper financial discipline for which as many as 27,000 officials were sanctioned. 'Let me make it clear to everyone present that our task is to improve financial management at every level of government', he said. Later that year, he again returned to the theme of budget inefficiency and imbalances, to point out that while a quarter of federal funding for housing and utilities was not being spent, other areas faced serious shortfalls.[13]

The second problem is the well-known and very prominent one of corruption. Opposition figures frequently publicise allegations of corruption at the highest levels in Russia: this was one of the main international stories of the Sochi Winter Olympics, for instance, and was at the heart of the public protests in March 2017.[14] Of course, the authorities usually dismiss such allegations out of hand as merely politically motivated accusations. Nevertheless, it is such a pervasive problem that some Russian observers have suggested that there is so much theft from the budget that the Ministry of Finance does not want to invest in projects.[15]

And the authorities themselves often acknowledge the systemic problems that corruption poses. These are extensive and stretch across the state's strategic agenda, and there are numerous examples that illustrate how corruption undermines the ability of the authorities to coordinate resources, placing a heavy additional burden on the budget. The depth and scale of the problem in the military is frequently emphasised: Sergei Fridinsky, the Chief Military Prosecutor, stated in 2011 that 20 per cent of the defence budget was being stolen: 'every year, more and more money is set aside for defence, but the successes are not great', with kickbacks and false contracts being used to defraud the state. 'The scale [of corruption] is sometimes staggering', he said, 'the sums of money stolen are shocking'.[16] Eighteen months later, the Prosecutor General's office reported that corruption in the military had increased by 450 per cent in a year,[17] and while it was severe in state defence procurement it was also evident in other sectors, including outsourcing and property management, as the Oboronservis scandal illustrated.

Putin and Medvedev have themselves often spoken of the problems that corruption poses – in 2009 Medvedev even suggested that officials 'almost openly' steal a significant portion of money apportioned to the North Caucasus. They also acknowledge that it strikes at the heart of the May Edicts: Putin has repeatedly stated that corruption hinders and even threatens Russia's national development prospects, and in 2013 pointed to it being the root cause of the failure to implement housing and utilities and construction plans. Putin himself emphasised that it was 'obvious to everyone' that the two main problems faced by Russia are nothing new: corruption and the low effectiveness of state power.[18]

Conducting the orchestra?

This leads to the second set of internal problems faced by the leadership in attempting to implement their plans – 'conducting the orchestra'. As Lawrence Freedman stated, successful strategy requires people to follow the script, and as soon as they deviate, problems emerge. For many observers in the Euro-Atlantic community, Putin is a 'KGB strongman' who brooks no dissent and maintains a firm, unopposed grip on power, including though his so-called 'vertical of power', which is often understood as a hierarchical chain of authority staffed by loyalists. And to be sure, he has not faced substantial organised political opposition. Nevertheless, this is only part of the picture, and the Russian authorities do face numerous obstacles in ensuring that people 'follow the script'. Indeed, there is much deviation from it.

One reason for this is that although the authorities have established an architecture for creating strategy, built around the Security Council, the 'orchestra' of ministries, agencies and other organisations is rarely harmonious. Putin has often explicitly noted how difficult it is to coordinate the federal, regional and local authorities on one hand, and, on the other, the various ministries. He has also repeatedly indicated his view that agencies 'look solely and exclusively to their own narrow problems and lack understanding of the common strategic tasks facing our country'. As a result, important objectives were effectively 'ignored'.[19]

This is in part, as Stephen Fortescue has argued, because of the problem of 'vedomstvennost' – ministries and agencies have strong vertical hierarchies, usually based on a particular sector, which claim the loyalty of all officials in that sector. Officials are usually technical experts in the ministry's area of responsibility, often working their way up through the ranks to ministerial level, Fortescue argues, and, as a result, they see the world in the technical terms of the agency that they run and this supplants wider loyalties to party or the state. Furthermore, signing off legislation is a weapon in bureaucratic politics, even tantamount to a veto, and used as an obstructionist tactic to defend or advance the ministry or agency's interests.[20]

This latter point is exacerbated because there are different policy priorities and disagreements, not to say rivalries, ministries and agencies, and even between the government and the presidential administration. Even within specific sectors such as law enforcement or the military, coordination is not always smooth. Pavel Baev has remarked that the Russian high command traditionally included two main superstructures, the Ministry of Defence and the General Staff, with 'overlapping responsibilities and competing authority, while the territorial system of military districts did not work in synch with the functional system of special commands for each branch of the armed forces'.[21] As a result, information is not shared, bodies do not coordinate well in their tasks, a piecemeal approach is adopted and policy deadlocks emerge. At the same time, lines of responsibility and final authority are not clearly delineated, with the result that some tasks either often overlap or gaps emerge – again, a shortcoming that Putin has explicitly repeatedly criticised for leading to 'failures in work'.[22]

One of the most important illustrations of these gaps in priorities and disagreements has been that over public spending, and particularly the gap between economic planning and defence spending. In 2011, this was one of the reasons that led to the resignation of the then long-standing Finance Minister Alexei Kudrin, who cited disagreements over economic policies, especially the high defence expenditure. Such gaps also feed back into the process of formulating the strategic agenda, significantly delaying both formulation and implementation: for instance, the law on strategic planning took eight years to pass, burdened by disputes between the federal centre and the regions, between economic and security budgeting and between those who advocated a greater role for state planning in the economy and those who opposed it.[23]

Finally, and more significantly still for our understanding of Russian strategy, despite the vertical of power, the country's leadership has long faced problems in having its instructions implemented. The vertical of power requires some brief background explanation. The origins of the vertical can be traced back to the early 1990s, but it is most often associated with the Putin era, and his attempt to create a hierarchical chain of authority to provide strong government from the top through loyalty, discipline and responsibility to fulfil tasks. According to Alexander Goltz, the urgent necessity for such a chain of command was made clear to Putin by the *Kursk* tragedy, since the military misled him as the tragedy unfolded.[24]

This work to improve the chain of command and create an integrated bureaucracy to enhance the manageability of the state apparatus has remained an important feature of Russian political life since then, including during Dmitri Medvedev's presidency (2008–12). One Russian observer suggested that the reshuffle of personnel in 2009 and 2010 and the appointment of 'technocrats' indicated the attempt to provide final arbitration 'to settle the endless disputes', the dissolution of regional bureaucratic plans while integrating and disciplining the bureaucracy and thus improve the state's managerial efficiency.[25]

But rather than substantially enhancing the chain of command, there is a wealth of evidence to suggest that the vertical was often dysfunctional in practice, with many presidential instructions going unfulfilled. In 2005, for instance, just 55 per cent of presidential instructions were fulfilled, falling to 45 per cent the following year, and there are many reports of reprimands and admonitions being administered by the top leadership ordering ministers to implement plans and instructions during Putin's first two terms as president.[26] As one US researcher pithily put it, therefore, in the early years of Putin's leadership, it was 'authoritarianism without authority', since Putin simply did not possess the political authority across Russia to implement reforms.[27]

A Russian editorial suggested in 2010 that even hand-picked officials are ineffective and often 'quietly sabotage the orders of the Prime Minister and President'.[28] Other observers suggested that the authorities faced a 'passive revolution' from a bureaucracy that passes instructions back up the chain of authority, that had become 'out of control' and, in practice, 'sovereign', imposing its will on the authorities.[29]

Official sources also admitted as much. Konstantin Chuichenko, head of the Main Control Directorate in the Presidential Administration, reported to Medvedev in June 2010 that the number of presidential instructions implemented on time had risen by 68 per cent, with the result that 20 per cent of all instructions were being implemented on time. Medvedev himself lamented that he often found himself signing orders that would change nothing, nor bring about anything new, simply re-iterate something already ordered.[30] And it should not be assumed that this is merely because it was Medvedev at the presidential helm, rather than Putin. Yulia Latynina, a prominent Russian journalist, suggested that even senior officials could not care less about Putin's instructions and that the elite does not listen to him much more than to Medvedev.[31]

This brief overview of the failings of the vertical of power, particularly when added to the other problems discussed above, illustrates the great difficulty the leadership has faced in having people, even those on its own side, 'follow the script'. The obvious underperformance in the implementation of plans and instructions is important because it has a dual effect for our understanding of Russian strategy. First, it means that the leadership has often struggled to respond even to major crises. In 2009, Medvedev criticised the government for its failure to implement more than 30 per cent of the measures announced to address the economic crisis.[32] In 2010 and 2011 Russia faced two major domestic crises: the spread of summer fires, the scale of which caused the government to call a state of emergency in seven regions; and major terrorist attacks on the Moscow Metro and at Domodedovo airport.

Both again revealed the problems in the chain of command. The fires revealed many of the same failures that it had been created to address – local authorities, including governors and senior military officers, maintained that the fires were under control, a deception that resulted in much damage. Speaking at an expanded Security Council meeting, Medvedev stated that the evidence from the investigation after the fires suggested a 'neglect of duty and criminal negligence'. Similarly, the attack at Domodedovo was followed by reports of senior officials deceiving the authorities. It transpired that measures introduced following the Moscow Metro bombing the previous year had not been implemented and the president's new orders to increase and improve security at major transport hubs were being ignored. Russian journalists remarked that the country was struck by a 'paralysis of governance'.[33]

Second, it reflects the limitations the leadership faces in setting an agenda and having it implemented: there were serious problems, for instance, fulfilling the 2010 and 2011 state defence orders. And on a visit to the Far East in 2013, Putin pointed to a maximum of 20 per cent of a development plan having been implemented, even though it had been developed with the regional authorities' own contribution and consent − and again, a journalist remarked that Putin's subordinates 'ignore his instructions unashamedly'.[34] The implementation of the May Edicts, the central strategic agenda, has been similarly problematic. Regarding the plans for the housing and utilities sector, Putin emphasised that just 4 per cent of the 2013 plans had been implemented. 'This is simply unacceptable', he said, 'this is not serious work'.[35] Thus, again, Russian journalists were suggesting that bureaucrats were ignoring the May Edicts, and using the phrase 'systemic sabotage' to describe the situation regarding the strategic agenda.

Russian observers therefore often talk of a crisis of administration, a problem publicly acknowledged by the leadership. The vertical of power, the means through which the leadership attempts to implement its policies and therefore the heart of Russian strategy, is often dysfunctional and only really works when it is micro-managed by the top leadership in what is known as 'manual control'. Russian observers have suggested that this need for manual control 'permeates all branches of government', that ministers and governors will not act until the president himself 'leads them by the nose' to the problem, mayors and district heads wait for instructions from governors and so on.[36]

Notes

1   R. Connolly, *Troubled Times: Stagnation, Sanctions and the Prospects for Economic Reform in Russia*, Chatham House Research Paper (February 2015), p. 5.

2 J. Cooper, 'Sanctions will Hurt Russia's Rearmament Plans', *Moscow Times* (12 August 2014), https://themoscowtimes. com/articles/sanctions-will-hurt-russias-rearmament-plans-38270. The annexation of Crimea and the concomitant crisis imposed a range of further economic burdens, including, among others, record capital outflow and adding the cost of Crimea to the federal budget.

3 'Poslaniye Prezidenta Federalnomu Sobraniyu', WPA (12 December 2013), http://kremlin.ru/events/president/news/ 19825.

4 C. Gaddy and B. Ickes, *Bear Traps on Russia's Road to Modernization* (London: Routledge, 2013), pp. 2–3, 96–7.

5 The domestic air network suffers from both an aging fleet of aircraft and a shrinking number of useable airports, since many local airports have closed or need major modernisation. The author is grateful to Julian Cooper for this point.

6 *Komsomolskaya Pravda* (18 October 2016).

7 C. Lo, 'Russian Railways: Connecting a Growing Economy', *Railway Technology* (1 May 2013), www.railway-technology.com/ features/featurerussia-railways-connecting-growing-economy/.

8 'Zasedaniye presiduuma Gossoveta po voprosu razvitiya vnutrennikh vodnykh putei', WPA (15 August 2016), http://kremlin.ru/events/president/news/52713. The author is grateful respectively to Nazrin Mehdiyeva and Richard Connolly for points on the energy sector and industry.

9 M. Barabanov, 'Russian Military Reform up to the Georgian Conflict', in C. Howard and R. Pukhov (eds), *Brothers Armed: Military Aspects of the Crisis in Ukraine* (Minneapolis: East View, 2014), p. 88.

10 This figure was indicated in the State Arms Programme to 2020 (approved in 2010), and covers only the arms programme, not the other costs of the Ministry of Defence.

11 '"Sabotazh" po-Ulyukaevsky', *Sevodnya* (3 December 2013), www. segodnia.ru/content/132197; 'Zasedaniye pravitelstva', Website of the Russian Government (12 September 2013), http://government.ru/news/4804/; 'Experty obsuzhdayut skolko nuzhno potratit

na mechtu Medvedeva po sozdaniyu "sobstvennovo Kipra" na dalnem vostoke', *Newsru.com* (22 March 2013), www.newsru.com/arch/finance/22mar2013/fareast_offshore.html; 'Ministers, Governors to be Fined for Failing to Implement Presidential Edicts', *ITAR-TASS* (31 January 2014), http://tass.com/opinions/763168. Putin responded by criticising the government, and saying that economic problems should 'mobilise the government'.

12   'Putin Demands Implementation of May Edicts Despite Regional Finance Problems', *Tass* (27 March 2014), http://tass.com/russia/725571.

13   'Zasedaniye Gosudarstvennovo soveta', WPA (4 October 2013), http://kremlin.ru/events/president/news/19359; 'Sovmestnoe zasedaniye Gossoveta i Komissii po monintoringu dostizheniya tselevikh pokazatelei razvitiya strany', WPA (23 December 2013), http://kremlin.ru/events/president/news/19882.

14   Until his murder in 2015, Boris Nemtsov had published several investigative texts into high-level corruption, including regarding the Sochi Winter Olympics. Today, Alexei Navalniy is the most prominent such figure. He established the Anti-Corruption Foundation in 2011 to 'investigate, expose and fight corruption among high ranking officials'. In March 2017, Navalniy accused Prime Minister Medvedev of amassing a multi-million dollar property portfolio. Some public protests ensued, while Medvedev and other senior figures dismissed the claims. 'Fond borby c korruptsiei' [Anti-Corruption Foundation], https://fbk.info/english/about/; 'Russia Dismisses Sweeping Corruption Allegations Against Medvedev', *Washington Post* (5 March 2017), www.washingtonpost.com/world/europe/russia-dismissessweeping-corruption-allegations-against-medvedev/2017/03/05/dac18d32–01af-11e7-a391–651727e77fc0_story.html?utm_term=.7a039535f054.

15   K. Smirnov, 'Putin spotknulsya o svoyu vertikal', *Moskovsky Komsomolets* (18 July 2013), www.mk.ru/politics/2013/07/17/885584-putin-spotknulsya-o-svoyu-vertikal.html.

16   'Masshtab korruptsii v rossiiskoi armii potryasaet dazhe glavnovo prokurora', *Newsru* (11 January 2011), www.newsru.com/russia/11jan2011/armycorruption.html; 'Oruzhie dayot "otkaty"', *Rossiiskaya Gazeta* (24 May 2011), https://rg.ru/2011/05/24/fridinskij.html.

17 'Corruption up 450% in a Year in Russian Military – Prosecutors',
    Sputnik News (11 July 2013), https://sputniknews.com/news/
    20130711182183954-Corruption-up-450-in-a-Year-in-Russian-
    Forces--Prosecutors/.

18 'Poslaniye Prezidenta Federalnomu Sobraniyu', WPA (12
    December 2012), http://kremlin.ru/events/president/news/
    17118; 'Poslaniye Prezidenta Federalnomu Sobraniyu', WPA
    (12 December 2013), http://kremlin.ru/events/president/
    news/19825.

19 'Prezidentu predstavleni plani raboti ministerstv po ispolneniyu
    maiskikh ukazov'.

20 Correspondence with S. Fortescue, April 2017. For more on
    'vedomstvennost', see S. Fortescue, 'The Policy-Making
    Process in Putin's Prime Ministership', in Lena Jonson and
    Stephen White (eds), *Waiting for Reform Under Putin and
    Medvedev* (Palgrave: Basingstoke, 2012). 'Vedomstvennost'
    might find its counterpart in 'departmentalitis' in the United
    Kingdom or the 'parochial Cabinet Member/Secretary' in the
    United States.

21 P. Baev, 'Crooked Hierarchy and Reshuffled Networks: Reforming
    Russia's Dysfunctional Military Machine', in V. Kononenko
    and A. Moshes (eds) *Russia as a Network State: What Works in
    Russia When State Institutions Do Not?* (Basingstoke: Palgrave
    Macmillan, 2011), p. 62.

22 'Zasedaniye priziduuma Gossoveta', WPA (29 November
    2012), http://kremlin.ru/events/president/news/16990.

23 Author's correspondence with Julian Cooper.

24 A. Goltz, 'Putin's Power Vertical Stretches Back to Kursk',
    Moscow Times (17 August 2010).

25 This is particularly noteworthy given the discussions in 2016
    and 2017 about Putin replacing 'charismatic' people with
    'technocrats'. M. Agarkov, 'Modernizatsiya vertikali', *Expert*
    (1 February 2010), http://expert.ru/expert/2010/04/moderni-
    zaciya_vertikali/.

26 See, for instance, 'Polpredstvo: na Urale ne ispolnyayut
    porucheniya prezidenta RF', *Rossiiskaya Gazeta* (21 July 2011),
    https://rg.ru/2011/07/21/reg-ural/porucheno-anons.html.

27   K. Stoner-Weiss, *Resisting the State: Reform and Retrenchment in Post-Soviet Russia* (New York: Cambridge University Press, 2006), pp. 147, 150.

28   'Vertikal loyalnosti', *Nezavisimaya Gazeta* (24 March 2010), www.ng.ru/editorial/2010–03–24/2_red.html.

29   Inozemtsev, 'Neo-Feudalism Explained'; R. Sakwa, *The Crisis of Russian Democracy: The Dual State, Factionalism and the Medvedev Succession* (Cambridge: Cambridge University Press, 2011), pp. 29–33.

30   'Kremlin Seeks List of Punished Officials', *Moscow Times* (24 March 2010).

31   'Roi, ili antibulochnik', *Novaya Gazeta* (25 January 2010); 'Zastupnik elity', *Ezhednevnyi Zhurnal* (14 January 2011).

32   'Speech at Expanded Security Council Meeting on Fire Safety Measures for Strategic Facilities', WPA (4 August 2010), http://en.kremlin.ru/events/president/transcripts/8570.

33   'Stranu khvatil paralich upravleniya', *Nezavisimaya Gazeta* (11 February 2011).

34   Smirnov, 'Putin spotknulsya'.

35   'Sovmestnoe zasedaniye'.

36   'Strane nuzhen glaz da glaza', *Izvestiya* (14 September 2010).

3

Making Russia work

A PICTURE of Russian grand strategy is taking shape. On one hand, a structured strategic planning architecture has slowly taken shape, and a set of regularly updated plans, even an ambitious strategic agenda, has been broadly, if somewhat unevenly, formulated. On the other, the implementation of this agenda throughout the 2000s was problematic, both because of the complex context in which Moscow was working and because of the difficulty of coordinating the necessary resources and conducting the orchestra. The reliance on manual control meant that power was being created only unevenly, in specific areas and at certain times – to be sure, some plans were being implemented well and in a timely fashion, particularly when directly attended to by the leadership, but others were only partially implemented or their implementation dragged out or largely ignored. This, and the way the authorities have sought to resolve it, is central to understanding Russian strategy and mobilisation.

Since the early 2010s, the Russian authorities have sought to accelerate some measures and introduce others to make the vertical function more effectively and implement their agenda. There is a strong sense of urgency about these measures because of the pessimism of the assumptions and therefore what the leadership sees as the unfavourable balance between an increasingly competitive global landscape and the difficult situation in Russia. Both Putin and Medvedev have repeatedly emphasised this. Medvedev stated in 2014, for example, that 'Russia is experiencing triple pressure for the first time'. This included global economic instability, the 'unfriendly policies of some leading countries', particularly the sanctions, leading to a 'deteriorated international environment' and 'internal structural limitations', he said, before noting that 'faced with this unprecedented challenge, it is crucial that we calmly stick to the strategy we have chosen'.[1]

This is the context in which Putin has emphasised that 'only by mobilising all the resources at our disposal both administrative and financial' that Russia would be able to respond to the grave long-term challenges that faced it,[2] and many Russian commentators were also suggesting that there was a 'mobilisation' feel to these measures.[3] This feeling was underlined by the substantial increase in defence spending from some 3.4 per cent in 2011 to 4.84 per cent in 2015 as Moscow prioritised defence expenditure and investment in the military industrial complex as a locomotive for the economy during a sustained and serious economic slowdown.[4]

A patriotic mass mobilisation?

For some this has meant that the leadership has sought to 'mobilise' the wider population behind an 'enemy at the gates' idea, one that encourages patriotism, even nationalism, and focuses attention on the external threat to rally the population, shore up support and divert attention from domestic problems. This form of 'mass mobilisation' is often referred to as the 'Crimea effect'. Andrei Kolesnikov, a prominent Russian journalist, has suggested it would be difficult to 'overstate the impact that war has made on the mass consciousness of the Russian public'. He says that the leadership is promulgating a sense of permanent war in messages that entwine glorified memories of the Great Patriotic War with contemporary threats. Moscow seeks, in his view, to foster a sense of Russia as a besieged fortress and to justify the interventions in Crimea and Syria as Russia waging pre-emptive war to avoid or prevent a bigger one, as defensive deployments. The leadership's continued grip on power, he argues, depends on the Kremlin's ability to sustain current levels of political mobilisation.[5]

Others, too, have pointed to the Russian leadership's attempt to rally support by combining propaganda and youth movements to prepare Russian society for the likelihood of future conflict, and so introducing a mobilisation mentality. According to one, the primary means the Russian leadership has used during the last five years to mobilise Russian society is the mobilisation of the information space. The consolidation of control over major media outlets, and the establishment of TV channels such as *Zvezda*, a station dedicated to covering military and patriotic topics, Ray Finch suggests, means that the leadership can portray their message in a 'consistent, persistent, coordinated and largely one sided manner', and 'drive home the point of mobilising for future battle'.[6]

Another Russian journalist, Alexander Baunov, also points to the various attempts the authorities have made to mobilise particular sectors of the population at different times, including through youth organisations such as Nashi, established in 2004 (and wound up in 2013), Molodaya Gvardiya and others, including Yunarmiya, a military-patriotic movement run from the Ministry of Defence.[7] Such organisations serve a number of purposes, including building loyal grassroots support and confronting opponents by meeting protest rallies with counter-demonstrations.[8]

To be sure, as discussed above, the authorities have painted a picture of a threatening and challenging environment, and these organisations have roles to play in the Russian sociopolitical landscape. And other moves, such as the agreement to establish cooperation between the Ministry of Defence and the Ministry of Culture to strengthen patriotic education and advocate military-history education including through domestic tourism might seem to be yet more evidence to confirm such a process.[9]

Even so, this is not 'mobilisation'. Indeed, it is not clear that the Russian authorities seek to mobilise the population at large, not least since a genuinely mobilised population might make demands on the leadership and become a transformative political force. Instead, socio-political efforts are targeted to specific purposes. As Wayne Allensworth, an experienced American Russia watcher, has suggested, therefore, this is a 'patriotic wave', rather than mass social mobilisation – emotion and a sense of passive support is different to mobilisation. While the mass of the Russian population may broadly support the leadership's policies passively, it does not mean that they are ready to fight for them. That the leadership understands this is indicated, Allensworth suggests, by the sense of secrecy shrouding Russian involvement in Ukraine – keeping the dangers of the war, and especially the casualties, hidden from the population. Thus, if Igor Strelkov, a prominent figure involved in the war in Ukraine, complained that not enough volunteers turned up to fight in Donbass, and too many were staying at home on the sofa drinking beer, this is ideal for Moscow, which does not want the masses to show up until the officially organised bus comes to mobilise them under specific circumstances for specific purposes.[10] In large part, this has meant making it impossible for the opposition to mount major anti-Putin political campaigns.

Kolesnikov similarly notes that the population remains 'skittish' about a real war. Therefore, the leadership has embraced a 'virtualisation' of war, one in which there are no significant losses on the Russian side and in which actual demands are not made of the population – the large majority of the population only experiences war through mass media. By 2016, he suggests, war had become routine, and yet actual demands are not made on the wider population.[11] This is an interesting echo of Mary Dudziak's argument noted in the Introduction about the *separation* of the wider population in the United States from the wars being fought by their government, where war has become 'normal life' for the wider population and in which there is no call to defend the state because war had become the government's task. This has long been a complex problem for Moscow and is a question to which we will return in Chapter 4 when discussing military reform.

Systemic mobilisation as grand strategy

We must return to the definition of mobilisation framed in the Introduction as a complex of state measures for activating the resources, strength and capabilities for the achievement of military-political aims, and practical measures for the transition to a war footing of the country's military, economic and state institutions. The mobilisation approach that Moscow has adopted is more focused on improving the effectiveness of the system, rather than mobilising a potentially restive population. It is focused on a series of initiatives that cut across the political and economic landscape.

This includes a slightly changed approach to the May Edicts. Although he has continued to maintain that they must be implemented, Putin appears to have accepted that they cannot be implemented on the basis of a strong economic performance. In its place, the leadership is emphasising greater efficiency, including cost-cutting and increasing responsibility for the implementation of plans, as well as measures to enhance the vertical of power. Yet another anti-corruption drive is under way, including in the defence sector, and a number of high-ranking officials, including in law enforcement, have been fired and prosecuted. Together, this represents an acceleration of already established procedures, but there are also some noteworthy new instruments and organisations that are altering the political and economic landscape in Russia.

First, the authorities have sought to create strategy by clarifying ministerial responsibility, strengthening the vertical of power and improving coordination by establishing new ministries. At the same time, the leadership has conducted an ongoing series of 'rotations' of senior officials, including in the economic sector and among presidential plenipotentiaries. Moscow has presented these moves as creating a better alignment of authorities – effectively reinforcing the vertical through linking the plenipotentiary, minister and regional governor – across strategically important regions and seeking enhanced efficiency in the use of resources in the fulfilment of the May Edicts.[12]

Furthermore, while Putin has in the past indicated his dislike of reshuffles and firing individuals, there has been a noteworthy increase in turnover of personnel since he returned to the Kremlin in 2012. Numerous governors have been dismissed, officially for having lost the confidence of the president, but particularly on the basis of failing to implement the leadership's plans, and some of them have been subsequently pursued on allegations of corruption. More noteworthy, though, is the number of ministers and other senior figures, even those close to Putin, who have been fired, resigned or retired – including Anatoliy Serdyukov (Minister of Defence), partly as the result of the Oboronservis corruption scandal, and others on the basis of Putin's unhappiness with their performance in implementing the May Edicts or inefficient use of resources. Oleg Govorun (Minister of Regional Development), Viktor Ishaev (Minister of Development of the Far East) and Vladislav Surkov (Deputy Prime Minister) all lost their positions by the end of 2013.[13]

Subsequently, some heads of Russian state companies, including Vladimir Yakunin (Russian Railways), Evgeniy Dod (RusHydro) and Vladimir Dmitriev (Vneshekonombank/VEB), have also lost their positions, apparently on the basis of their profligate use of resources. VEB, for instance, had sought another huge financial bailout just prior to Dmitriev's dismissal, and Putin had publicly criticised Dod in 2013 for failing to recoup money overspent on contractors and subsequently fired him in 2015.[14]

The leadership has also sought to improve manual control measures by altering the structure of major meetings. This is not a new process, and some background is worth noting. While he was prime minister, Putin attempted to overcome 'vedomstevennost' and streamline government decision-making by rehabilitating the practice of appointing a number of first deputy and deputy prime ministers tasked with resolving policy differences between ministries and agencies. Deputy prime ministers were empowered to give directives to whichever ministry or agency was involved in a specific policy issue, even if it lay outside the deputy's sector.

Putin also introduced gatherings called 'soveshaniya'. These were distinguished from the various more formal councils and commissions because they were used as small, informal gatherings as a form of log-jam busting, as consultation and decision-making fora, largely replacing formal decision-making bodies to resolve deadlocks. Though they were not initially devised for dealing with crises, they proved more useful formats as part of the crisis management policy-making when the economic and financial crisis broke out almost immediately after their introduction in 2008.[15]

This background is important because of the success and therefore continued use of 'soveshaniya' even during crisis times, as well as the subsequent introduction of similar but more formal and regularised extended government meetings. Since 2013, Putin has chaired these broader meetings the more closely to monitor and control the implementation of the May Edicts, and held regular enlarged government meetings – in effect, seeking to provide direct oversight over the vertical of power and thus tighter over the implementation of plans and instructions. Such meetings bring together representatives from the presidential administration, government, specific agencies, relevant regional heads and business interests to pursue specific questions across various sectors in detail. In the defence sector, for instance, regular meetings bring together state officials and military-industrial complex representatives.

A number of other bodies have been also established to contribute to strategy by generating ideas and helping to implement them, such as the Agency of Strategic Initiatives, and, in summer 2016, the Strategic Development and Priority Projects Council. Speaking at the Strategic Development and Priority Projects Council's inaugural meeting, Putin stated that its purpose was to bring people together and 'become the centre for finding solutions for structural transformation in the economic and social sphere'. It would seek to set the main directions for accelerating economic growth and social development. He emphasised that it was 'crucial to continue our work to reach the objectives set out in the May 2012 Presidential Edicts'. The council's job was to 'set tasks, identify solutions and oversee project implementation'.[16]

Perhaps the most important of these, however, is the All-Russian Popular Front (ONF). Established in May 2011 as a civil volunteer organisation, the ONF was intended to build a link between the authorities and society, but its role has substantially evolved and it is now playing an increasingly important role in Russian strategy. In June 2013, it became an officially formalised movement with its own bureaucracy, and is now established nationwide across Russia, with members in senior positions in ministries and in parliament.

Officially, the ONF's remit, laid out in its charter, is very broad: to promote unity and civil solidarity, and Russia's development as a free, strong and sovereign state, or, as the website also puts it, to promote 'love of the Fatherland, strengthening the state and embracing social welfare and justice'.[17] It had a dual political role to play, both providing a political platform for Putin during the elections of 2011–12, and consolidating social consensus beyond the ruling United Russia (UR) party by co-opting different parts of the wider political landscape under its broad umbrella. When it was established, therefore, the ONF's role was to serve as a public platform to capture the wide range of support for the authorities that did not fit easily into the main party structure, or vote for UR, and even bring in some opposition. In other words, UR might poll (in 2011) at some 50 per cent, while Putin would gain 80 per cent approval ratings, and the ONF's role was to capture that 30 per cent gap.[18]

But there are a number of important tasks also mandated in the charter relating directly to Russian strategy. At his regular meetings with the ONF, Putin has often pointed to the movement's important role in both formulating and implementing plans, and its remit has broadened significantly, now including employment and housing and utilities, healthcare, education and transport infrastructure, particularly the quality of roads. Speaking to the ONF's Action Forum in November 2014, for instance, he stated that many of the ONF's ideas and proposals had been adopted first into the president's Federal Assembly speech and then into government resolutions.

Indeed, the May Edicts, Putin continued, were ' "our" executive orders' because they were 'born out of extensive work of early 2012 when the ONF made an analysis of the problems facing Russia',[19] and in 2016 at an inter-regional forum, he said that such meetings help the government and presidential administration to formulate policies, draft amendments to federal laws and propose new laws. Furthermore, as Silvana Malle notes, given the position of ONF members in the parliament, the movement has played a role in shaping legislation relating both to banning the use of foreign internet servers by state agencies and state-related agencies, and also to 'de-offshorisation', which came into force in January 2015, seeking to stem (and even repatriate) the outflow of capital that some suggest hit US$200 billion in 2014.[20]

The ONF's role in implementation of the leadership's plans, especially the May Edicts, also appears to be increasing, particularly in terms of scale of the organisation's operations – some 14,000 people were involved in monitoring the implementation of instructions by 2015. The two primary approaches are through its 'For Fair Procurement' activities against waste and corruption, including in the defence sector, which resulted in the creation of an index of wastefulness of state authorities and companies, and its monitoring of the activities of regional officials – and submitting complaints to the leadership, which are dealt with by the Main Control Directorate in the Presidential Administration and the law enforcement organs. The ONF's monitoring activities appear to have contributed to the firing of several officials noted above, since their complaints about corruption or ineffectiveness (or both) have led to the dismissal of a number of governors (and their replacement with senior members of the ONF) and to adjustments in programmes and government expenditure to the tune of 227 billion rubles (some US$3.5 billion at the time).[21]

This broad remit now goes beyond attempting to enhance resource efficiency to include import-substitution programmes, the reinvigoration of domestic industry and coordinating with the Transport Ministry to work on road development plans.[22] Indeed, as Malle suggests, the creation of the ONF reflects a significant change not only in Russian politics, but also in the economic sector. In April 2015 Putin introduced the concept of 'economic sovereignty' at the ONF's media forum: 'asserting economic sovereignty as an economic policy objective was a warning to those beyond the Forum's audience that Russia would undertake any effort to strengthen her security and independence', Malle suggested, 'not from foreign trade ... but from unfriendly countries that had resorted to sanctions against Russia a year earlier'.[23]

Economic security

This phrase 'economic sovereignty' leads us to the measures the Russian leadership has introduced in the economic sector. Indeed, there has been an important shift underway since 2010 as security has come to dominate economic thinking and policy, and Moscow's attempt to ensure both the resilience and self-sufficiency of the economy is leading to a number of structural and organisational changes in the economic sphere, particularly in the financial and defence industry sectors. These are intended to insulate Russia from hostile foreign economic measures and cope with potential and actual threats. This was reiterated in the National Security Strategy published in 2015, which states the need for economic security in the face of the threats posed by the economic statecraft being used by other states.

Richard Connolly suggests that this reflects the leadership's attempt to refit the Russian economy to be able to withstand conflict, and is particularly noteworthy in terms of financial security and import substitution. An awareness of vulnerabilities in the financial sector has led to a series of measures to address this, including the construction of a new national electronic payment system that replaces the SWIFT payments system, the creation of domestic credit ratings agencies and the development of a new domestic card payment system that can replace Visa and

MasterCard. The purpose of these measures is not economic efficiency but to make Russia economically more resilient and less vulnerable to foreign influence and 'economic statecraft'.[24]

The emphasis being placed on import substitution by the leadership reflects the significant change of direction that has taken place. In 2009, Putin was reluctant to engage in wide-ranging import substitution. But by 2015, Dmitri Medvedev stated that import substitution is Russia's strategic priority, a point codified in the National Security Strategy. The document is explicit in its statement that the implementation of an import substitution programme and the reduction of the critical dependence on foreign technology and industrial production is a key objective. Areas identified include military production, pharmaceutical products, the energy industry and agriculture-industrial production, and the programme is supported by significant state resources including tax breaks, state-subsidised cheap credit from VEB and the fund for the development of industry. Again, Connolly remarks that the import substitution campaign represents a 'core component of a wider state-directed effort to enhance Russia's sovereignty and economic security' and reducing Russian dependence on imports is now a key component of national security.[25]

Many problems remain. Despite the 'soveshaniya' and enlarged government meetings in focusing attention on specific points and improving the implementation of plans, there are still shortfalls. If the state defence order was being fulfilled by the middle of the decade, and Putin stated that the defence industry meetings had led to 150 of 200 orders now being implemented, that still, of course, left 25 per cent unimplemented, even with his direct oversight.

For the May Edicts, the picture is mixed. In 2014 parliamentarians asserted that even official figures accepted that only one in fifteen of the May Edicts were being implemented. Their implementation, if done at all, was only on paper, they argued, and one group sought to prepare criminal legislation proposing legal responsibility for the failure to fulfil presidential instructions – with the concomitant proposal to not just fire those guilty of sabotage but to impose fines or even lengthy prison sentences.

Though they appear, perhaps unsurprisingly, to create resentment in the regions, the monitoring activities of the ONF do seem to result in more active oversight. Alexander Brechalov, a senior figure in the movement, told Putin in late 2014 that while by quantity the May Edicts appeared to be on track, the implementation was qualitatively poor, and less than 20 per cent of the targets were being met.[26] While the criminal legislation proposal was finally abandoned in October 2015, parliamentarians and the ONF were still emphasising that large parts of the May Edicts were still not being fulfilled, and journalists on state television suggested that the debate about the failure to implement the May Edicts did not really address *why* they were not being implemented, since the reasons were obvious: a lack of money, a lack of competence among officials, bureaucratic foot-dragging and maybe corruption, and the broader difficulty of the overall situation.[27]

On the fifth anniversary of the Edicts in spring 2017, the government reported that 76 per cent of the orders had been fulfilled, but observers again pointed to the gap between the claimed fulfilment percentage on paper and the 'more modest practical results'.[28] Putin himself indicated the ongoing ambiguity when he said that:

> over these last years, we have set positive change in motion in the areas of most importance for our people's life ... of course there are still many problems and more outstanding issues than problems resolved. But implementation of the executive orders has reinforced the partnership between the state authorities at all levels and civil society to reach our national goals. The public supervision system the ONF organised has substantially raised effectiveness.[29]

Economically, there are also obstacles, both in terms of devoting the necessary resources to the intended ambitions during a time of continued pressure on the budget and in ensuring sufficient focus on specific measures such that resources are not spread too thin. Resilience measures are unlikely to reach fruition until the 2020s, and even then achieving sovereignty and self-reliance is likely to be uneven and restricted to certain areas.

Nevertheless, the overall point about Russian grand strategy remains – the leadership is imposing pressure on the system to make it more effective and resilient. Russia's political and economic model is focused on reducing vulnerability and emphasising consolidation and security, rather than liberalisation and economic efficiency, and there is an evolution underway in the structure of the political and economic landscape in Russia.

Notes

1   'Government Report on its Performance in 2013', Website of the Russian Government (22 April 2014), http://government.ru/en/news/11875.

2   'Enlarged Meeting of Government', Website of the Russian Government (31 January 2013), http://archive.government.ru/eng/docs/22596/.

3   'Putin gotovitsya k mobilizatsii', *Lenta.ru* (12 May 2014), http://lenta.ru/articles/2014/05/12/putinnaz; 'Mobilizatsiya bez shoka', *Expert* (14 July 2014); 'MinFin vnyos v pravitelstvo mobilizatsionnyi byudzhet', *Vedomosti* (17 September 2014).

4   J. Cooper, 'Prospects for Military Spending in Russia to 2017 and Beyond', 31 March 2017, www.birmingham.ac.uk/Documents/college-social-sciences/government-society/crees/working-papers/prospects-for-military-spending-in-Russia-in-2017-and-beyond.pdf.

5   A. Kolesnikov, *Do Russians Want War?*, Carnegie Report (June 2016), pp. 1–2, http://carnegieendowment.org/files/Article_Kolesnikov_2016_Eng-2.pdf.

6   R. Finch, 'The Mobilisation of Russian Society', Special Essay, *OE Watch*, Vol. 6, No. 11 (November 2016), p. 63.

7   Launched in May 2016, by spring 2017 it had some 100,000 young members across Russia, Website of the Ministry of Defence, http://mil.ru/youtharmy/info.htm.

8   A. Baunov, *Going to the People and Back Again: The Changing Shape of the Russian Regime*, Carnegie Report (January 2017), http://carnegieendowment.org/files/CP_292_Baunov_Russian_Regime_Web.pdf.

9   'Minoborony i Minkultury obiedinyat usiliya v patrioticheskom vospitanii', *Interfax* (16 February 2017), www.interfax.ru/Russia/550239.

10 Correspondence with the author, April 2017.

11 Kolesnikov, *Do Russians Want War?*, pp. 1, 2, 6.

12 'Putin napomnil polpredam o maiskikh ukazakh. Eti dokumenty stanovyatsya novoi ideologiei Kremlya', *Nezavisimaya Gazeta* (10 April 2014); 'Kavkaz: Sibirskoe uskoreniye', *Rossiiskaya Gazeta* (13 May 2014).

13 Equally, it should be noted that their firing was not 'terminal' – both Serdyukov and Surkov have been appointed to new positions, Surkov returning to a post in the Presidential Administration. For more on the rotation, personnel turnover and the emergence of new figures, see Monaghan, *The New Politics of Russia*, chapter 4.

14 'Putin Removes Head of VEB State Development Bank as Crisis Bites', *Reuters* (18 February 2016), www.reuters.com/article/russia-veb-idUSL8N15X2UO; 'Update 2-Ex-Boss of Russian State Firm Charged with Fraud', *Reuters* (22 June 2016), http://uk.reuters.com/article/russia-onexim-quadra-idUKL8N19E31X. Dod was subsequently arrested on charges of fraud.

15 Correspondence with Stephen Fortescue, April 2017. Also see Fortescue's 'The Policy-Making Process in Putin's Prime Ministership'.

16 'Zasedaniye Soveta po strategicheskomu razvitiyu i prioritetnym proyektam', WPA (13 July 2016), http://kremlin.ru/events/president/news/52504.

17 Website of the All-Russian Popular Front, http://ONF.ru.

18 Monaghan, *The New Politics of Russia*, pp. 108–9, 112.

19 'Forum deistvii Obshcherosiiskovo narodnovo fronta', WPA (18 November 2014), http://kremlin.ru/events/president/news/47036.

20 S. Malle, 'The All-Russian National Front – For Russia: A New Actor in the Political and Economic Landscape', *Post-Communist Economies* (2016), pp. 11–12.

21 'Forum deistvii Obshcherosiiskovo narodnovo fronta', WPA (22 November 2016), http://kremlin.ru/events/president/news/53289.

22 'Mediaforum regionalnykh i mestnykh SMI "Pravda i spravedlivost"', WPA (3 April 2017), http://kremlin.ru/events/president/news/54172.

23 Malle, 'The All-Russian National Front', p. 8.

24 R. Connolly, 'Towards Self Sufficiency?', *Russian Studies Series*, NATO Defence College (July 2016).

25 Ibid., pp. 6–7; R. Connolly and P. Hanson, *Import Substitution and Economic Sovereignty in Russia*, Chatham House Research Paper (June 2016).

26 'ONF zayavil o nevypolnenii 80% poruchenii Putina', *Polit.ru* (18 November 2014), http://polit.ru/news/2014/11/18/onf_80/.

27 'Ni odin iz maiskikh ukazov prezidenta ne vypolnen', *Nezavisimaya Gazeta* (3 April 2014); News Report, *Russia 24* (23 December 2015), www.youtube.com/watch?v=2qsZDJTS6yk. The parliamentarian Evgeniy Fyodorov suggested that even on official figures, only 25 per cent of the May Edicts had been implemented, www.youtube.com/watch?v=QaXp-1ZzLiA. 'Sabotazh ne nakazuem: V Dume otklonili vvedeniye ugolovnoi otvetstvennosti za neispolneniye ukazov prezidenta RF', *Novorosinform* (13 October 2015), www.novorosinform.org/news/39213.

28 'O chom umolchalo pravitelstvo v otchyote o maiskykh ukazakh', *RBK* (5 May 2017), www.rbc.ru/economics/05/05/2017/590b5f449a794702ed8d31f2?from=subject.

29 'Sovmestnoe zasedaniye Gossoveta i Komissii po monitoringu dostizheniya tselevykh pokazatelei sotsialno-ekonomicheskovo razvitiya', WPA (4 May 2017), http://kremlin.ru/events/president/transcripts/54448.

4

Defending Russia

THE sense of mobilisation and pressure on the system, and thus the attempt to generate grand strategy, is all the more tangible in the security and military realms. Indeed, because of the 'changing geopolitical situation' and the 'spread of instability and conflict', since 2013 senior officials have spoken of the urgent need for the armed forces to reach a 'fundamentally new capability level within three to five years', and of developing measures to prepare Russia's transition to a war footing. In December 2016, for instance, Putin stated clearly that mobilisation preparedness is an important part of the overall effort to ensure Russia's security.[1] Again, the impact of the events in Ukraine and North Africa and the Middle East is explicit in Russian thinking, as is the concern about the possibility of a major conflict as a result of increasing competition over influence and resources.

And Gerasimov's 2013 article offers useful insight into the thinking of the Russian leadership about evolving security concerns – not least since he offered some reflections on mobilisation. He quoted the Soviet-era military theoretician Georgii Isserson first to note that 'war in general is not declared, it simply begins with already developed military forces', before concluding 'mobilisation and concentration is not part of the period after the onset of the state of war, as in 1914, but rather *unnoticed, proceeds long before that*'.

The historical roots of Russian mobilisation that are relevant for today can be briefly encapsulated in two points. On one hand, it is about complex administration – the storing and moving of equipment and supplies, the coordination, organisation and concentration of resources, personnel and transport, and their subsequent deployment. On the other, it is about how the Russian leadership thinks about the evolution of war, and the balance between the nature and character of war – what features remain essentially constant, and what changes with time, technology and so on. As a result, mobilisation is associated both with modernisation of the armed forces and security of the nation and, related to that, readiness to face challenges as the leadership seeks to establish the kind of force structures required to resolve weaknesses and maximise advantages. Mobilisation can therefore be understood in both practical and theoretical terms, and is about understanding the evolution of war and implementing measures to face it.

This has two further practical elements. First is concern in Moscow about a 'mobilisation gap'. This arises from a dual unease occasioned by the balance between Russia's size and limited infrastructure (and comparative military shortcomings) and the superiority of infrastructure and capabilities of an adversary. The gap accentuates concerns about Russian weakness: both the administrative complexities of organising, concentrating and deploying forces and the possibility that enemy forces might be able to achieve the upper hand by organising and deploying their own forces faster would mean that the adversary would gain a rolling strategic advantage in the conflict.

Given such an advantage, the adversary would enjoy a 'compound initiative' – in which initiative increasingly enables further accelerating advantage. Russia's own mobilisation could be disrupted by a faster adversary, with the consequence that the adversary would enjoy numerical advantage in battle, likely winning these early encounters and thus having the opportunity to fragment command and control and decision-making.

Related to this is the ongoing debate in the Russian armed forces about structure, particularly the need for large armies in modern war and the difficulty of economically sustaining them. During the Soviet era, the answer to this question was the cadre mobilisation system, in which, during peacetime, units would be kept at skeleton strength only to be brought up to full strength when mobilisation was declared. This system was designed for fighting major wars, and reflected more traditional forms of 'defence of the motherland' type of mobilisation through volunteers and conscription – a demand on the citizens to make sacrifices in service of the country.

But as Mikhail Barabanov, a prominent Russian expert on military matters, has suggested, the Russian leadership has since the collapse of the USSR faced a 'mobilisation crisis' in which the national mobilisation-centric armed forces were inappropriately structured to be deployable to contemporary problems. Though government-ordered mass mobilisation would generate serious public opposition and protest, the leadership faced limited local wars and conflicts that still demanded at least partial mobilisation – which then led to protests. The practical result of this was that for most of the post-Cold War era the government had an intractable problem: domestic political conditions meant that the leadership could not mobilise armed forces to respond effectively to local conflicts, but due to internal pressure from parts of the military, a shift away from mass mobilisation structures was not possible since they were deemed to be essential to defending Russia in case of a large war. Any internal concessions to a professional force were limited and slow in bearing fruit.

The question for the leadership, therefore, was how to retain a mass mobilisation-centric establishment, while managing to use available forces effectively in limited conflicts without invoking mobilisation. This dilemma has dominated Russian military reform, informing debate about force structure and numerical size, and command and control. The result, however, was a haphazard balancing act which sought to maintain a professionalised, combat-ready and deployable armed force in parallel with a much larger and effectively undeployable mass mobilisation structure, all while having very limited resources to maintain even part of this dual force. Any spending, therefore, even when it was increased, was spread very thin across the armed forces and thus had only very limited effect. The practical consequence was that for most of the post-Soviet era, the Russian armed forces have been both increasingly obsolete and of limited capability and use. This debate is ongoing and, as discussed below, how the leadership has sought recently to address it is revealing about twenty-first century mobilisation.

These themes of readiness, capability and deployability go to the heart of how the Russian leadership sees the world and is attempting to meet it. As noted above, Moscow's concerns about an evolving and contested international environment include the potential for colour revolution in Russia and in its neighbouring states, the threat posed by terrorist armies, and growing competition through the next decade including the increasing use of modernised armed forces by leading states. As a result, a notable transformation in Russian security and military capabilities is underway, under emergency conditions – a decade-long transition period to rebuild and re-equip the armed forces, the establishment of major new structures and the testing of the effectiveness of the security establishment in thousands of exercises.

Reform and re-equipment of the armed forces

The Russian armed forces are undergoing an intensive period of reform and re-equipment. Following the Russo-Georgia war in 2008, the Russian leadership instigated what Barabanov has called the 'most radical military reform since the creation of the Red Army following the 1917 Bolshevik Revolution'. The speed and depth of reforms under Anatoly Serdyukov, who was Defence Minister from 2007 to 2012, were striking, including considerable downsizing both in terms of personnel and structure, the reorganisation of the central command structures and education, the introduction of new military districts, a shift to brigade structure and the transformation to a combined recruiting system. Underpinning these reforms was the aim to move away from the concept of the mass mobilisation of reserves towards a combat-ready force consisting of contracted professionals.[2]

And as noted in Chapter 1, since 2010, the Russian authorities have sought to implement an extensive investment and arms procurement programme. Moscow's procurement list is a long one, including equipment for sea, land, air and space. While many in the Euro-Atlantic community have focused on the non-military aspects of 'hybrid warfare', it is important to take stock of what is included in this list, because the emphasis in the 2010 state arms programme is very much on the acquisition of firepower. The nuclear arsenal is scheduled to receive 400 intercontinental and submarine-launched ballistic missiles, eight nuclear-powered ballistic missile submarines, and Tu-160 and Tu-195MS long-range bombers are to be modernised. Other equipment to be procured includes 100 military satellites, 700 modern fighter aircraft, 1,000 helicopters, 56 S-400 air defence battalions, 2,300 tanks, 2,000 self-propelled and tracked artillery pieces, 20 attack submarines and 50 combat ships. The May Edict also includes the intention to modernise air-space defence, electronic warfare capabilities, intelligence and control systems, unmanned aviation equipment, modern military transport aviation, robotic strike systems, high-precision weaponry and individual soldier defence systems.

Senior defence officials have emphasised that modernising the military and acquiring state-of-the-art weaponry is a vital condition for Russia's existence, and despite the economic stagnation, defence spending has remained comparatively high – protected, even – to ensure the acquisition of the necessary capabilities. That is not to say that there are no problems and delays, as discussed below, but to be clear about the high priority being accorded to this agenda.

The reform and modernisation of Russia's military also involves the establishment of new structures and organisations, including the re-constitution of the 1st Guards Tank Army and the establishment of the Arctic Joint Strategic Command in 2014, and, in August 2015, the Russian Aerospace Forces through the merging of the air force and the aerospace defence forces. Two others stand out because of their state-wide role.

Reshaping the Russian security landscape

The first reflects the attempt to improve command, control and management across Russia. At the heart of this is the National Defence Management Centre (NDMC) in Moscow. Built in 2014, it was, according to senior generals, a particular priority. The NDMC is a major – and overdue – upgrade of the Central Command of the General Staff, with numerous new features and roles. Gerasimov confirmed the existence of the project in May 2013, stating that it would provide a centre that would unify all existing command and monitoring systems across Russia and act as the single main point of coordination for information and control over all agencies in Russia. It also monitors and coordinates major exercises and monitors arms procurement and communications. In wartime, it would assume control of Russia, issuing orders to all ministries, agencies, state companies and other organisations.[3]

General Mikhail Mizintsev, the commander of the NDMC,[4] has said that the closest analogy in terms of the NDMC's function is the Commander-in-Chief Headquarters during the Second World War, which 'centralised all controls of the military machine and the economy of the nation in the interests of the war'. He also emphasised that the NDMC would be based on three different levels of command. The supreme command centre at the highest levels of the country's political-military command deals with strategic nuclear capabilities. At the second level, a combat command centre monitors the global politico-military situation, provides analysis and forecasting of the development of threats to Russia and its allies, and through which military operations would be run. And the third level is the centre of everyday activity, coordinating the work of security ministries and departments in peacetime – the NDMC connects every military unit, and officers can, in real time, monitor and communicate with units thousands of miles away. He added that the organisation's control extends well beyond the Ministry of Defence's remit to include command and control of all military forces, including special formations and organs. The NDMC's importance, according to

Mizintsev, lies in the fact that in today's world, it is necessary for the armed forces to be ready to react quickly without a transition period to a war footing: the NDMC provides the capability to do so.[5]

The NDMC is also tasked with other roles: it is equipped with a supercomputer that facilitates, for instance, strategic analysis and forecasting, drawing on material from past wars to assess how future wars might evolve. Shoigu has used the example of the war in Yugoslavia. He suggested that it was

> a large-scale NATO operation. Their naval buildup, missile deployment, dislocations and distances were all subject to analysis. The machine tells us that this or that situation is 90% similar to what happened in Serbia, then we know that this is likely to happen again and take appropriate measures.[6]

The computer, which is based on domestically produced hardware, is also used to collate all cyber threats identified by Russian forces and agencies, according to Mizintsev, coordinating the work of the Interior Ministry (MVD), Foreign Intelligence Service and Main Intelligence Directorate (GRU). It provides IT security for Russian military institutions, as well as the Foreign Ministry and Kremlin, as well as monitoring social networks to prevent extremist propaganda, civil unrest and violent anti-government protest.

The NDMC is at the heart of a national network of such centres, that now spread out into the regions, and, as Julian Cooper has suggested, it can be regarded as a 'central innovation of the drive to enhance the readiness and effectiveness of Russia's military capability and to integrate its various strands, including mobilisation planning'. Indeed, it seems that the NDMC is prepared to play the central role in Russian mobilisation in the case of national emergency or war, providing decision-making coherence and speed and overseeing, coordinating and managing its practical implementation.[7]

The other major new structure is the National Guard (NG, also known in Russia as Rosgvardia). The NG was established in April 2016, and confirmed in Federal Constitutional Law by Putin in July. The law's provisions state that it is intended to 'enhance the guarantee of national and public security', including the 'protection of human and civil rights and freedoms' and controlling the 'trade and circulation of arms', that the president is responsible for the NG's activities, and that the NG is one of the forces that the authorities can call on in the event of a state of emergency.[8]

The NG has a dual function. The first involves civil disobedience management. The Kremlin's spokesman, Dmitri Peskov, has stated that the NG will engage in the enforcement of public order and participate in anti-terrorism operations.[9] Altay Krai's regional NG commander suggested at a public briefing that the structure was established to combat revolutionary ferment and a 'fifth column', particularly in the shape of public organisations funded from abroad,[10] though Alexander Khinshtein, an advisor to Viktor Zolotov, the NG's director, replied that the organisation's tasks are clearly stated in the legislation, and that there is no mention of revolutionary ferment.[11] Nevertheless, in early 2017 Sergei Melikov, the first deputy commander, reiterated that:

Rosgvardiya sees its role not in dispersing meetings but in pre-empting negative conditions in which the mass discontent of citizens reaches the level of mass disobedience ... As a rule, behind the mass of people who go onto the streets stands a small group of inciters who conduct destructive work. So we have to isolate such plotters and arrest the inciters.[12]

The NG represents a major reorganisation of Russian internal security forces, and consists of Russian interior troops and various special forces, including riot police and rapid reaction forces, and coordinates its activities with other law enforcement structures from the Interior Ministry, the Federal Security Service, the Investigative Committee and the Procurator General. It is also a part of the Council of Chief Designers for General Purpose Forces, bringing it together with the Military-Industrial Commission, the Ministry of Defence and the Ministry of Industry and Trade.

Certainly, given the forces of which it consists, Rosgvardia is a substantial and heavily-armed force, some 340,000 strong, according to official sources, and equipped with armoured vehicles, heavy artillery, automatic weapons and attack helicopters.[13] Indeed, Dmitri Rogozin, Deputy Prime Minister in charge of the defence industry, has stated that since the NG is always in action, it should be 'armed to the teeth' with modern weapons, including high-precision capabilities.[14]

Rehearsing mobilisation

Alongside the reform, re-equipment and establishment of new structures, many thousands of exercises have been conducted. These have taken three main forms: civil defence and emergency management, policing and military. Since 2012, the Emergency Ministry (MChS) has held annual nationwide civil defence exercises. In October 2016, a three-stage drill was held to practice 'organisation and management during civil defence events and emergency and fire control'. The exercise involved 200,000 service personnel and over forty million people nationwide, and was intended, according to Vladimir Puchkov, Emergencies Minister, to test coordination between federal, regional and local authorities, and responses to natural and man-made disasters, including fire safety and radiation, chemical and biological leaks and evacuation and the deployment of monitoring and sanitisation centres.[15]

There have also been regular strategic policing exercises. The eight-day 'Zaslon-2015' exercise, for instance, held across six Russian regions, tested the readiness of the police, MVD and paramilitary formations to respond to a 'colour revolution'-type scenario. Vasily Panchenkov, the MVD's spokesman, stated that the exercise was 'based on the events that took place in the recent past in a neighbouring country and featured all the attributes of those events' – a clear reference to the Maidan events in Kyiv.[16] The exercises involved joint operations to seal the borders, countering civil disobedience and ensuring law and order, and to ensure territorial defence, counter-terrorism and the protection of strategic installations.

Other policing and internal security exercises have taken place based on similar scenarios. In April 2016 exercises were held in the Moscow region of Lyubertsy and in Smolensk to rehearse controlling mass demonstrations. The exercises in Smolensk were focused more on unauthorised social protest, based on an increase in municipal services charges. The authorities appeared to rehearse a version of kettling, separating the crowd with barbed wire and arresting ringleaders.[17] Rosgvardia has also begun to conduct exercises. In summer 2016, it coordinated with airborne assault forces in the Volgograd region to train to extinguish internal armed conflict,[18] and in April 2017 it held its first major combat readiness tests. Beginning in the Central Federal district, before spreading into other districts, the exercise was intended to test Rosgvardiya's readiness to combat saboteur and reconnaissance groups and terrorist and extremist formations, as well as working through and practising mobilisation preparedness. A particular focus was the security of strategically important energy, industry and transport sites.[19]

Finally, the military has been through thousands of exercises and snap inspections at federal, regional and local levels. These have been designed to test combat readiness and responsiveness, as well as coordination between civil and military, and federal and regional authorities. These have grown considerably in size and sophistication, including both combined and joint operations. Johan Norberg, a prominent Swedish expert on the Russian military, is unequivocal in his views of these exercises: by 2015 'Russia had been preparing its armed forces for a regional confrontation with possible escalation into using nuclear weapons for at least four years'. Consequently, the Russian armed forces were 'most likely capable of launching large-scale conventional high-intensity offensive joint inter-service operations, or ... to put it simply, to conduct big war fighting operations with big formations'.[20]

These exercises and inspections have had numerous purposes, including mobilisation rehearsal, but two stand out. First, they have focused on fast deployments across long distances, and drawing together the military forces of the entire country. The Vostok exercises in 2014, the largest in many years, practised combat training and long-distance deployments, marches with heavy weapons and regrouping, and the use of long-distance precision weapons. Exercises in the West have taken on a similar scale: in March 2015, just before the Zaslon-2015 exercise discussed above, the military conducted a major snap inspection to test the combat-readiness of the northern fleet and its reinforcement from the Central, Southern, Western and Eastern Military Districts. Led by Gerasimov himself with Deputy Minister of Defence General Dmitry Bulgakov, the exercise also included the deployment of strategic rocket forces and long-range aviation, airborne forces and marines.[21]

Second, Shoigu has stated that the exercises are also about checking the performance of mobilisation systems across Russia. They have extended well beyond the military and security organs, and focused on enhancing command and control, particularly coordination between civilian and military agencies and ministries, and federal, regional and local levels. The Main Directorate for Special Projects (GUSP) has played an important role in these exercises. Led since 2015 by Alexander Linets, formerly the head of the Federal Security Service in the Southern Military District, GUSP oversees the implementation of mobilisation preparation.[22] The exercises can be said, therefore, to have been rehearsing the whole state's capacity to wage modern war.[23]

The Kavkaz-2016 exercise was a good example. The exercises focused on territorial defence, drawing on divisions from four armies and deploying them long-distance and coordinating them with command units in a new theatre of operations. It also explicitly tested regional mobilisation readiness, and involved coordination with the Ministries of Industry and Trade, Communications and Finance, the Central Bank and Bank of Russia and elements of the defence industry. Furthermore, it was the first real-time test of the Ministry of Defence taking direct control over regional and local authorities, police, security and Rosgvardia, and the emergency services. This tested the new rules of wartime administration which give all administrative powers to the military.[24]

Problems remain. As Barabanov has noted, the radical nature of the reforms 'inevitably put Serdyukov on a collision course with vested interests among the top brass', and the attempt to shift to a professional armed force has faced persistent internal opposition. With Serdyukov's removal in 2012 and his replacement by Shoigu, there has also been a shift in emphasis. As a result, although the trajectory has remained broadly consistent, there have been some policy U-turns, including shifts back to a mixed system of conscripts and contracted professional non-commissioned officers and a partial return to divisions, a growth in the officer corps and the reversal of the education reforms. Alexander Goltz has suggested that the 'generals continue to sabotage every order from the top that they dislike'.[25]

The reserve system remains problematic, and despite the restructuring of the armed forces, the mechanisms for 'maintaining and mobilizing the military reserve still look very vague and haphazard', and how units are to replace combat losses during limited conflicts also remains unclear.[26] The military authorities undermined plans to encourage conscripts to join the reserves voluntarily on completion of their mandatory national service because they continue to view the whole Russian adult male population as the reserve. They also resisted Shoigu's plan to offer a form of military service to army-age university students and thus gain 80–100,000 extra reservists every year.[27] At the same time, Shoigu has maintained that he is on target to reach the stated number of contract professionals in the armed forces, reaching nearly 400,000 in 2016.[28]

Furthermore, the arms procurement list and the time-frame for its achievement is ambitious. It is optimistic in terms of how quickly the Russian defence industry can produce new equipment, and assumes 'no delays, technical or design problems or bottlenecks'.[29] Initially, progress was slow, and there are ongoing delays in delivery of equipment. Even though there has been a significant increase in funding directed towards procurement and the modernisation of the defence industry, much ground had to be made up in conditions of corruption and spending inefficiency. And, as noted above, the modernisation process was affected by the loss of access to the Ukrainian defence industry and Western sanctions on dual-use technology. Producing new advanced weapons systems has proved difficult, and the modernisation process has largely meant the upgrading of Soviet-designed equipment.

Notwithstanding such questions, informed Russian and Western observers agree that there is good progress in modernising the Russian armed forces, albeit from a rather low level. The target for the modernisation of equipment appears to be within reach: in spring 2017 Putin indicated that the share of modern weapons and equipment across the armed forces had reached some 58 per cent by the end of 2016, and that all the conditions were in place to reach 70 per cent by 2020. He also indicated some progress on replacement of imported engines, suggesting that the delays may be shorter than originally anticipated.[30]

Finally, there are ongoing problems in operational efficiency and preparedness. In July 2016, the command team of the Baltic Sea fleet was fired, apparently on the basis of incomplete combat-readiness in the fleet, even in newer ships, which meant that they could not be deployed, and a failure to implement the parts of the May Edicts relating to service conditions. The official statement also indicated that the commanders were misrepresenting the situation in their reports – illustrating ongoing failings in the working of the vertical.

And, as they were intended to, the many snap inspections have revealed problems in logistics, transport and reconnaissance and communications,[31] and the coordination of federal, regional and local authorities and civilian and military sectors. Russian media indicated that Shoigu had criticised many officials, particularly the governor of Sakhalin, Alexander Khoroshavin, for not being ready for times of war and not summoning reserve forces quickly enough. He requested, therefore, that Putin order federal officials, governors and mayors to attend instruction and training courses on mobilisation preparedness and regional governance during mobilisation periods at the General Staff Academy.

Russian media suggested that the General Staff considered civilian officials to be unready for Vostok-2014 and, as a result, to have performed poorly during the exercise. An unnamed General Staff source indicated that 'regional authorities often fail to understand the importance of military exercises and prefer to drag their feet in executing orders because they simply do not know what they should do and how they should do it'.[32] Shortly afterwards, Khoroshavin was relieved of his duties as governor and then arrested on bribery charges, accusations in which the ONF appear to have played a role.

Putin himself pointed to this problem, saying:

> [mobilisation] should be the responsibility of the regional heads, but they seem to see it as being of secondary importance ... territorial defence is the responsibility today of various agencies and is not centralised at all. We need to raise the regional heads' responsibility in this area too ... [but] we often encounter an inadequate reaction to our efforts to defend our national interests.[33]

Subsequently, a series of measures have been introduced. Parliamentarians have undergone training courses on combat-readiness with Rosgvardia. In late 2016, legislation was prepared on the establishment of territorial defence staffs to be led by governors and other local civilian authorities to facilitate coordination between the organs of regional and military authorities in the move to a war footing and mobilisation activities. Russian media noted that this appeared to be a lesson from the situation in Ukraine, where the Ukrainian authorities could not respond to the localisation of the conflict in Donbass. And in February 2017, Putin signed a law that introduced personal responsibility for federal ministers, governors, municipal heads and the heads of local authorities for regional mobilisation measures in wartime.[34]

So the transition process remains flawed and incomplete. Nevertheless, the Russian armed forces have attempted to begin a transformation away from old mass mobilisation towards a more modern form of combat readiness and capability to cope with a modern array of threats, real and perceived, based on the leadership's assumptions. Progress is being made, and the national security picture is already transformed. Even in 2014, Breedlove suggested that the Russian armed forces were able to demonstrate 'unexpected flexibility in moving their forces significant distances, achieving readiness very rapidly and man-oeuvring to preserve a variety of options. This degree of agility and speed is new and something we have to adapt to'.[35] The intervention in Syria demonstrates the continuation of this tran-sition, as does the evolving capability of the NG (due to be com-pleted in 2018), and its involvement in internal security action against terrorists.

Notes

1   'Rasshirennoe zasedaniye kollegii Ministerstva oborony', WPA (27 February 2013), http://kremlin.ru/events/president/news/17588; 'Soveshanie po voprosam mobilizatsionnoi gotovnosti OPK', WPA (17 November 2016), http://kremlin.ru/events/president/news/53263; 'Genshtab poluchil dopolnitelniye pol-nomochiya, podgotovil plan perekhoda RF na usloviya voen-novo vremeni', *Newsru* (25 January 2014), www.newsru.com/arch/25jan2014genshtab.html.

2   M. Barabanov, 'Changing the Force and Moving Forward After Georgia', in Howard and Pukhov, *Brothers Armed*; A. Goltz, 'The Inherent Limits of Russian Military Reform: Another Lost Opportunity', in *Russia's Military. Assessment, Strategy and Threat* (Washington, DC: Center on Global Interests, June 2016).

3   'V Rossii sozdayut Natsionalniy tsentr upravleniya oboronoi', *Izvestiya* (28 May 2013), http://izvestia.ru/new/551033; 'Prikaz postupit iz tsentra', *Rossiiskaya Gazeta* (27 October 2014), www.rg.ru/2014/10/27/kartapolov.html.

4   Mizintsev has extensive operational command experience. He was head of operational command and deputy chief of staff in the North Caucasus from 2010 to 2011, before becoming deputy chief of staff in the Southern Military District. In August 2012, he was appointed head of the central command of the General Staff, the predecessor organisation to the NDMC. In February 2017, Putin promoted him Colonel General, a Lieutenant General or 3-star level in Euro-Atlantic ranking, for service during the Syrian campaign. Website of the Ministry of Defence, http://structure.mil.ru/management/details.htm?id=12000953@SD_Employee.

5   'Mgnovennaya gotovnost', *Lenta.ru* (29 November 2014), http://lenta.ru/articles/2014/11/29/ntsuo.

6   Shoigu cited in 'Russian "Pentagon": RT Unveils Mysteries Behind Walls of Russia's MoD Management Centre', *RT* (3 February 2017), www.rt.com/news/376123-russia-defense-ministry-glimpse/.

7   Cooper, *If War Comes Tomorrow*, pp. 40–1.

8   'Podpisan zakon, napravlennyi na sovershenstvovanie voprosov obespecheniya gosudarstvennoi i obshestvennoi bezopasnosti', WPA (4 July 2016), http://kremlin.ru/acts/news/52330.

9   Peskov cited in 'Kremlin: National Guard Likely to be Involved in Suppression of Unauthorised Mass Actions', *Tass* (5 April 2016), http://tass.com/politics/867506.

10 'Komandir Rosgvardii: eyo sozdali dlya borby s revolyutsionnymi brozheniyami', *Medusa* (16 December 2016), https://meduza.io/news/2016/12/16/komandir-rosgvardii-v-altayskom-krae-nas-sozdali-chtoby-sderzhivat-revolyutsionnye-poryvy.

11 Zolotov is a long-term ally of Vladimir Putin. He served as head of the presidential security service from 2000 to 2013, when he was appointed first deputy Minister of the Interior, commanding the Interior Ministry's Internal Troops. For Khinshtein's comment, see https://mobile.twitter.com/Khinshtein/status/809779421783670788.

12 'Melikov utochnil zadachi Rosgvardii', *RIA Novosti* (3 February 2017), https://ria.ru/defense_safety/20170203/1487134178.html.

In July 2016 Putin appointed Sergei Melikov first deputy director. Melikov has extensive experience in counter-terrorism. From 2002 to 2008, he commanded the Felix Dzerzhinski (special operations) Division of the Interior Ministry's troops, whose tasks included protecting public order in Moscow and the Moscow region, to fight terrorism and extremism and the protection of major installations in wartime. In 2011, he was appointed commander of the Interior Ministry's troops in the North Caucasus, and in 2014 he was appointed Presidential Plenipotentiary to the North Caucasus.

13 'Gvardiya – vperyod', *Rossiiskaya Gazeta* (4 April 2016), https://rg.ru/2016/04/05/formirovat-nacgvardiiu-budut-na-baze-vnutrennih-vojsk-mvd.html.

14 'Rogozin predlozhil "do zubov" vooruzhit Rosgvardiyu', *Rossiiskaya Gazeta* (9 February 2017), https://rg.ru/2017/02/09/vice-premer-rogozin-predlozhil-do-zubov-vooruzhit-rosgvardiiu.html.

15 'Large-Scale All-Russian Civil Defence Drill to Take Place from 4 to 7 October', *MChS website* (3 October 2016), http://en.mchs.ru/mass_media/news/item/32915549.

16 Panchenkov cited in 'Russian Troops Practise Quelling Ukrainian-Style Revolution', *Telegraph* (9 April 2015), www.telegraph.co.uk/news/worldnews/europe/russia/11525385/Russian-troops-practise-quelling-Ukrainian-style-revolution.html.

17 'V Smolenske politsiya provela ucheniya v usloviyakh massovikh besporyadkov', *Novaya Gazeta* (23 April 2016), www.novayagazeta.ru/news/2016/04/23/121045-v-smolenske-politsiya-provela-ucheniya-v-usloviyah-massovyh-besporyadkov; A. Goltz, 'Gromit i ne pushchat' [To Bash and Restrain], *Ezhednevny Zhurnal* (25 April 2016), www.ej.ru/?a=note&id=29600.

18 'Pod Volgogradom voiska podavili ataku terroristov', *Nezavisimaya Gazeta* (1 August 2016), www.ng.ru/politics/2016–08–01/1_volgograd.html.

19 'V Rosgvardii provoditsya vnezapnaya proverka boevoi gotovnosti', Website of Rosgvardia (13 March 2017), http://rosgvard.ru/ru/news/article/v-rosgvardii-provoditsya-vnezapnaya-proverka-boevoj-gotovnosti.

20   J. Norberg, *Training to Fight: Russia's Major Military Exercises, 2011–2014* (Stockholm: FOI, 2015), pp. 61–2.

21   See 'Russian Eastern Military District Getting Ready for Strategic Exercise', *Sputnik News* (20 April 2014), https://sputniknews. com/voiceofrussia/news/2014_04_20/Russian-Eastern-Military-District-getting-ready-for-strategic-exercise-3484/; 'Novoe strategicheskoe komandovanie na base severnovo flota podverglos vnezapnoi proverke', *Vedomosti* (17 March 2015); 'Ministr oboroni Rossii general armii Sergei Shoigu provyol zaslushivanye o khode vnezapnoi proverki boegotovnosti', Website of the Ministry of Defence (18 March 2015), http://function.mil.ru/news_page/country/more.htm?id=12010701@egNews.

22   See www.gusp.gov.ru, and for (very) brief biographical details of Linets and the command structure, see www.gusp.gov.ru/pages/gusp/3729/3776/. Despite its importance to the mobilisation process – and thus Russian strategy, this organisation has hardly featured in Western discussions, probably because its activities are usually highly classified and require detailed research. An exception is Cooper, *If War Comes Tomorrow*, pp. 33–5, who also gives some history of GUSP's role in the Soviet era.

23   This point has also been made by Norberg, *Training to Fight*, p. 62.

24   'TsB voennovo vremeni', *Gazeta* (29 August 2016), www.gazeta.ru/army/2016/08/29/10165451.shtml.

25   For more discussion on this point, see A. Monaghan, *Russian State Mobilisation: Moving the Country on to a War Footing*, Chatham House Research Paper (May 2016), www.chathamhouse.org/publication/russian-state-mobilization-moving-country-war-footing.

26   M. Barabanov, 'Changing the Force and Moving Forward After Georgia', in Howard and Pukhov, *Brothers Armed*, pp. 120–1.

27   V. Mukhin, 'Rezervistam dadut komandu v sentyabre', *Nezavisimaya Gazeta* (20 July 2015); A. Goltz, 'Army Brass Sabotaging Putin's Plans', *Moscow Times* (27 July 2015).

28   'Rasshirenoe zasedaniye kollegii Ministerstva oborony', WPA (11 December 2015), http://kremlin.ru/events/president/news/50913.

29   M. Martens, *Russian Military Modernisation*. General Report of the NATO Parliamentary Assembly's Science and Technology Committee (11 October 2015), p. 4.

30   Even so, delays have accumulated and Putin has acknowledged that import substitution in the defence industry still has a long way to go. 'Zasedaniye voenno-promyshlennoi komissii', WPA (25 April 2017), http://kremlin.ru/events/president/news/54368; R. Connolly and C. Sendstad, 'Russian Rearmament: An Assessment of Defence Industrial Performance', *Problems of Post Communism* (October 2016), pp. 13–14; M. Kofman, 'The Russian Military a Force in Transition', in A. Goltz and M. Kofman, *Russia's Military: Assessment, Strategy and Threat* (Washington, DC: CGI, June 2016), and Goltz, 'The Inherent Limits of Russian Military Reform'.

31   'Zasednaiye voenno-promyshlennoi komissii', WPA (26 January 2017), http://kremlin.ru/events/president/news/53782.

32   'Soveshanie po voprosam razvitiya Vooruzhonykh Sil', WPA (12 November 2015), http://kremlin.ru/catalog/keywords/91/events/50675; 'DM Shoigu Asks Putin to Launch Obligatory Military Training for All Russian Governors', *RT* (25 November 2014), www.rt.com/politics/208551-russia-governors-military-training/.

33   'Rasshirennoe zasedaniye kollegii Ministerstva oborony', WPA (19 December 2014), www.kremlin.ru/events/president/news/47257.

34   'Deputaty i senator proshli kurs boevoi podgotovki ot Rosgvardii', *Izvestia* (20 February 2017), http://izvestia.ru/news/666220; 'Gubernatorov postavili v boevoi stroi', *Nezavisimaya Gazeta* (25 November 2016), www.ng.ru/politics/2016–11–25/1_6869_gubernatory.html; 'Putin utverdil vvedenie otvetstvennosti ministrov i gubernatorov za mobilizatsiyu grazhdan', *Nezavisimaya Gazeta* (22 February 2017), www.ng.ru/news/572743.html?print=Y.

35   P. Breedlove, 'The Meaning of Russia's Military Campaign Against Ukraine', *Wall Street Journal* (16 July 2014).

Conclusions: mobilising power in Russia

S O where does this leave us regarding our opening questions about Russian grand strategy? Four points stand out. First, the Russian leadership has a strategic agenda. A structured process, with the Security Council at its heart, has taken shape from the mid-2000s, albeit slowly and with difficulty, resulting in the overhaul of Moscow's strategic planning. A cascade of documents and initiatives indicating Moscow's intentions across a great range of subjects has resulted. There are still gaps, shortfalls and delays, and they are often overtaken by events. Nevertheless, these are standard difficulties for all strategic planning, rather than a particular failing of *Russian* grand strategy, and Moscow seeks to overcome the latter problem through the regular structured updating of the plans.

International audiences usually focus on the National Security Strategy and the Foreign Policy Concept as the key documents. And they are important, indicating Moscow's assumptions about international affairs and disagreements with the Euro-Atlantic community. But more attention should be paid to the Defence Plan, the preparation by the Security Council of strategic forecasting for a twelve-year period, a working document to be updated every six years,[1] and the new Economic Security Strategy published in 2017. More important still are the May Edicts, which have represented the leadership's agenda since 2012: this is to modernise Russia – effectively, to drag the country into the twenty-first century. Ambitious, aspirational and flawed though it may be, Moscow has a purposeful set of ideas based on a consistent set of assumptions.

Second, Russian grand strategy does not lie in Moscow's goals or even its agenda, but in its *execution*. It is in the vertical of power. It is a commonplace in the Euro-Atlantic discussion about Russia to assume that the vertical of power is well established, even that Putin has created a vertical of power 'unlike any we have seen in other great nations', allowing him to centralise authority and make quick, unopposed decisions. Similarly, it is widely believed that Putin controls all assets of national power in a seamless linking of state power.

As the Russian authorities themselves frequently acknowledge, however, the vertical is often dysfunctional. Even beyond the difficult context in which it operates, the 'orchestra' of Russian power is rarely harmonious or seamless, and there is much evidence that the leadership's direct instructions are tardily or partially implemented – often only when the leadership uses direct oversight and 'manual control'. As Freedman suggests, the problem with strategy is other people, both adversaries and those on your own side: strategy requires people to follow the script – as soon as they deviate, problems emerge. And in Russia, deviation from the script has been a frequent problem. While Vladimir Putin is a centrally important figure, in Russian politics, therefore, there is also a need to look beyond him to understand better the wider Russian political landscape.

The broader picture of Russian grand strategy, therefore, is mixed. For much of the 2000s, it was deeply flawed – while the persistent attempt to generate it was visible, inconsistent planning processes stumbled over weak or defective implementation mechanisms, such that there was effectively no Russian grand strategy. Even as the planning processes became more consistent, implementation remained a serious problem. But since the 2010s, a transformation has been underway. This is largely because of how Moscow sees the evolving international context and how this relates to the domestic situation within Russia itself. Effectively, the assumptions suggest that Moscow sees the emergence of growing challenges for which Russia is not ready.

This leads to the third point: the assumptions that influence strategic thinking and planning. These reflect concerns about a range of threats, real and perceived, including colour revolution and international terrorism and increasing competition between major states over resources and influence that is believed to be likely to continue, even accelerate into the 2020s – perhaps resulting in a major war.

This has driven what are a series of emergency measures to attempt to ensure that Russia is ready to face the tests posed by this challenging international environment. These are tantamount, as Russian officials and observers often suggest, to mobilisation. Mobilisation is, therefore, grand strategy in emergency circumstances: a complex of state measures for activating the resources, strength and capabilities for the achievement of military-political aims, including practical measures for the transition on to a war footing of the country's military, economic and state institutions.

This sense of a transition to a war footing has been visible through the attempt to make the state system function more effectively, to attempt to render the economy resilient to the threat of 'statecraft' by foreign adversaries, and the attempt to modernise Russia's military and security capability. This appears not as a traditional mass mobilisation, but instead as a more modern form of mobilisation, one which has some echoes of Western approaches to warfare. These include the greater focus on a surge capability in arms production and the *disentangling* of the population from war-fighting – treating it as a passive consumer of security on which tangible demands are not made because of concerns about mass protest. This dovetails with the explicit and repeated emphasis on state preparation during peacetime and *readiness* as a central theoretical and practical feature of mobilisation.

Fourth, this consolidation process is transforming the Russian political and security landscape as new organisations have been established, including Rosgvardia, the ONF and the NDMC. The latter two have implications for our understanding of Russian strategy, given their prominent roles in the formulation and implementation of plans and conducting the orchestra.

In consequence, the birth of a new Russian grand strategy is visible, ambiguous, troubled and uneven though it may be. Generating grand strategy is always difficult, but Moscow's attempt is purposeful, security focused, and proving successful in some areas. There are clearly still problems: the attempt to introduce resilience into the economy prioritises security over economic innovation and efficiency, but faces a number of obstacles, and problems remain in the implementation of the strategic agenda and coordination. Even now not all follow the script. But the modernisation of the military and security apparatus, which of course is a feature of that agenda, has seen considerable, if incomplete, improvement. Russia is some two-thirds of the way through a planned decade-long transition and to understand this, more attention should be paid to the shape of the overall trajectory.

The implications of this trajectory are obviously important for the Euro-Atlantic community. The war in Ukraine and Russia's intervention in Syria have provoked much discussion about Russia's resurgence in international affairs, its militarisation and confrontational policies. For many, Moscow's actions represent an aggressive challenge to the democratic international order, a revanchist, belligerent and strategically competitive approach that poses a serious threat to NATO and its member states.[2]

The argument here about Russian grand strategy does not disagree with this sense of challenge to the Euro-Atlantic community – indeed, the Russian leadership often makes explicit its many disagreements with the West, both in values and policies, as well as Moscow's belief that the world is entering a 'post-West' stage of development.

But it does shade it in different colours, pointing to the sense of grand strategy as a process and transformation underway in Russia. At the grand strategic level, the first point to make is a reminder that Russian grand strategy is about *Russia*, not the Euro-Atlantic community. At its heart has been an attempt to make up for the lost decade of the 1990s, both to modernise Russia and to consolidate the state and enhance its resilience. While the emphasis of the strategic agenda is largely on domestic measures, the Russian ship of state is also being prepared to head into what Moscow forecasts will be the troubled waters of a conflict-prone decade in the 2020s. There will be no substantive change in Moscow's direction until its assumptions change or targets, such as the modernisation of the armed forces, are (broadly) met, when it will evolve.

To be sure, plans will continue to be either diluted by the Russians themselves deviating from the script, or curtailed by limits on the availability of and competition over resources, or warped by the fog and friction of the wider context and the opposition of events. But the bigger trajectory that Moscow has set is likely to remain broadly consistent, with regular (evolutionary) updates of major planning documents, and reflected in the development of 'Strategy 2030', which is already underway, and perhaps in future election campaign articles.

This also provides a clear foundation on which to understand more specific Russian *strategies*, whether in Syria, towards the Euro-Atlantic community or elsewhere. Detailed awareness of both the bigger agenda and more specific plans will mitigate some of the strong sense of surprise about Russian actions. And important questions include: who is departing from the script? How does the vertical of power function – and what effect does 'vedomstvennost' have on implementing it? How does fog and friction affect Russian actions as plans meet reality?

At the same time, the Euro-Atlantic community's actions will have only a limited effect on this because the core agenda is primarily Russia-focused and seen as necessary modernisation and consolidation. Attempts to ease the tensions in the relationship will not lead to a significant softening of Moscow's policies, though an explicitly much tougher approach to Russia, or more assertive action and the deployment of force in Europe or other regions may accelerate it.

The second point is that Russian capabilities are already significantly evolving. Over time, as this evolution continues, Moscow's calculus of what can be achieved, and how, will change. Much of the Euro-Atlantic community's discussion about Russian grand strategy centres on the binary point of whether it is offensive or defensive. Such simple binary categorisation is unhelpful. At the broadest level, Russian grand strategy is defensive and likely to remain so for the immediate future – the primary goal is the protection and defence of Russian sovereignty, independence and territory, making Russia a modernised hub in Eurasia ready to cope with the challenges and demands of the next decades of the twenty-first century.

Defensive does not mean passive, though, and senior Russian officials have already indicated that the line between defensive and offensive (but not, in their view, *aggressive*) operations are blurring, just as the line between war and peace is blurred. Gerasimov has stated, for example, that during a defensive operation, in some directions, 'preventive, active, offensive actions are planned for', as has been learned from Russia's experience in Syria.[3]

Putin, too, has indicated that one of the mistakes that Moscow has made over the last twenty-five years was a failure to assert its national interests. 'We should have done that from the outset', he suggested, 'then the world would be more balanced'.[4] As Russian capabilities grow through the rest of this decade and beyond, Moscow may well seek to correct that 'mistake', and activities in defence of what Moscow sees as its national interests are likely to be more visible, even pronounced; indeed, Russia's intervention in Syria gives a good indication of how such capabilities may be used – Moscow sees this expedition not as stumbling into a quagmire, but as the comprehensive application of force allowing Russia qualitatively to change the situation in Syria. At the same time, Russia is establishing itself in the Arctic region, and already appears to be active in Afghanistan, and Egypt and Libya, as well as deploying substantial naval and air assets further afield.

By the 2020s, there will still be a balance between Russian strength and weakness, but the results of mobilisation will mean that Russia will pose a very different proposition to the Euro-Atlantic community. This may well serve to highlight the disagreements, including in the Euro-Atlantic area itself, such as NATO enlargement and ballistic missile defence.

To cope with this, it is time to recalibrate our understanding of Russia, going beyond the focus on Putin himself, important though he is, and looking beyond the so-called 'hybrid methods', which are essentially tactical and operational. It is necessary to move towards a more sophisticated grasp of the creation of power, how the state does (and does not) work and why, and the broader implications of the birth of a new Russian grand strategy. The lens of state mobilisation helps to tailor a view of how the Russian leadership sees the world, what it is trying to achieve, and how. To borrow a Russian phrase, it may not be pretty, but it is becoming increasingly effective.

Notes

1   'Sovbez RF podgovit strategicheskii prognoz Rossii na period bolee 12 let', *Interfax* (16 March 2017), www.interfax.ru/russia/553854.

2   'Michael Fallon and James Mattis Strike Hawkish Tone on Russia', *Financial Times* (31 March 2017).

3   'Na Yugo-Zapadnom napravlenii', *Krasnaya Zvezda* (15 September 2016), www.redstar.ru/index.php/component/k2/item/30426-na-yugo-zapadnom-napravlenii.

4   'Intervyu nemetskomu izdaniyu Bild Chast 1', WPA (11 January 2016), http://kremlin.ru/events/president/news/51154.

Further reading

Much has been written on the wider subject of grand strategy. Important works include Lawrence Freedman's *Strategy: A History* (Oxford: Oxford University Press, 2013), Beatrice Heuser's *The Evolution of Strategy: Thinking War from Antiquity to the Present* (Cambridge: Cambridge University Press, 2010) and Colin Gray's Oxford University Press 'strategy trilogy', including *The Strategy Bridge: Theory for Practice* (2010), *Perspectives on Strategy* (2013) and *Strategy and Defence Planning* (2014). Hew Strachan's *The Direction of War: Contemporary Strategy in Historical Perspective* (Cambridge: Cambridge University Press, 2013) concisely sets out the various meanings of strategy and its role in contemporary affairs.

For Russian views of strategy, a core text is Alexander Svechin's book *Strategy* (Minneapolis: Eastview, 1992), which Colin Gray has suggested 'bears comparison' with Carl von Clausewitz's book *On War*. Andrey Kokoshin is a leading contemporary Russian thinker on grand strategy. His books *O strategicheskom planirovanii v politike* [On Strategic Planning in Politics] (Moscow: URSS, 2007) and *Politiko-voennie i voenno-strategicheskie problemy natsionalnoi bezopasnosti Rossii i mezhdunarodnoi bezopasnosti* [Politcal-Military and Military-Strategic Problems of Russia's National Security and International Security] (Moscow: HSE, 2013) are not available in English, but his *Soviet Strategic Thought, 1917–1991* (London: MIT Press, 1998) is.

Two English-language works that examine Russian (imperial) grand strategy are William C. Fuller's *Strategy and Power in Russia, 1600–1914* (Oxford: The Free Press, 1992) and John P.

LeDonne's *The Grand Strategy of the Russian Empire, 1650–1831* (Oxford: Oxford University Press, 2004). Henrikki Heikka's *The Evolution of Russian Grand Strategy: Implications for Europe's North* (Polsis Paper, Birmingham, 2000), Ingmar Oldberg's *Russia's Great Power Strategy Under Putin and Medvedev* (UI Occasional Paper 1, 2010), and Andrey Tsygankov's 'Preserving Influence in a Changing World: Russia's Grand Strategy', *Problems of Post-Communism*, Vol. 58, No. 2 (March–April 2011) all explore post-Cold War Russian strategy in different ways. Dmitry Adamsky's *Cross-Domain Coercion: The Current Russian Art of Strategy* (IFRI Proliferation Papers 54, November 2015) is another useful work.

Little work in English examines Russian strategic planning in detail, particularly beyond specific foreign and security questions, though an online series of articles, 'Russian Studies', published by the NATO Defence College (and edited by this author) includes detailed reviews of several of the major Russian strategic documents, www.ndc.nato.int/research/research.php?icode=6. Thomas Remington's *Presidential Decrees in Russia: A Comparative Perspective* (Cambridge: Cambridge University Press, 2014) is also useful.

Similarly, assessment of whether the vertical of power functions as a chain of command largely has to be gleaned directly from Russian language sources. Nevertheless, two important works on Russian domestic politics that discuss relevant questions are Richard Sakwa's *The Crisis of Russian Democracy: The Dual State, Factionalism and the Medvedev Succession* (Cambridge: Cambridge University Press, 2011) and Alena Ledeneva's *Can Russia Modernise? Sistema, Power Networks and Informal Governance* (Cambridge: Cambridge University Press, 2013).

Insightful work on Soviet-era Russian military strategy and mobilisation includes David Glantz's book *The Military Strategy of the Soviet Union: A History* (London: Frank Cass, 1992), which has a useful appendix on Soviet mobilisation in the Second World War. Chris Donnelly's book *Red Banner: The Soviet Military System in Peace and War* (London: Jane's Information Group, 1988) explores the shaping of the Soviet military mind, the roots of Russian political and military traditions and how the Soviet military machine worked, including command and control, mobilisation and the roles of social and youth activities.

The main work that explores economic aspects of Soviet-era mobilisation is Lennart Samuelson's *Plans for Stalin's War*

Machine: Tukhachevskii and Military-Economic Planning, 1925–1941 (London: Macmillan, 2000). Julian Cooper's *If War Comes Tomorrow: How Russia Prepares for Possible Armed Aggression* (London: RUSI, Whitehall Report 4–16, August 2016) offers detailed insight into a range of aspects of Soviet and contemporary Russian mobilisation, and is particularly good on economic matters.

Usually, Russian international security and military affairs and domestic politics are treated separately from each other and there is little substantive published work in English on the ONF or Rosgvardia. Robert Horvath's *Putin's Preventive Counter-Revolution* (London: Routledge, 2013) offers a good introduction to Moscow's efforts to counter colour revolution, and William Zimmerman's *Ruling Russia: Authoritarianism from the Revolution to Putin* (Princeton: Princeton University Press, 2014) includes reflections on Soviet-era and contemporary socio-political mobilisation.

The Swedish Defence Research Agency, FOI, regularly publishes good analysis of Russian defence industry and military capability, including Julian Cooper's *Russia's State Armaments Programme to 2020: A Quantitative Assessment of Implementation 2011–2015* (March 2016) and Gudrun Persson (ed.), *Russian Military Capability in a Ten-Year Perspective* (2016), as does the Foreign Military Studies Office (FMSO) in Fort Leavenworth, Kansas, such as Timothy Thomas's book *Russia: Military Strategy: Impacting 21st Century Reform and Geopolitics* (2015). All three texts are essential reading.

Index

Note 'n.' after a page reference indicates the number of a note on that page.